Early Childhood Units for Math

SCHOENBAUM LIBRARY
UNIVERSITY OF CHARLESTON

Written by Sandra Merrick

Illustrated by Keith Vasconcelles and Sue Fullam

Teacher Created Materials, Inc.
P.O. Box 1040
Huntington Beach, CA 92647
©*1993 Teacher Created Materials, Inc.*
Made in U.S.A.

ISBN 1-55734-200-8

The classroom teacher may reproduce copies of materials in this book for classroom use only. The reproduction of any part for an entire school or school system is strictly prohibited. No part of this publication may be transmitted, stored, or recorded in any form without written permission from the publisher.

Table of Contents

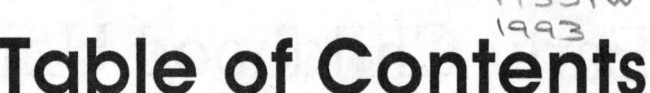

Introduction 2

What Is Whole Math? 3

Presenting a Whole Math Unit 4

Using the Patterns 5

How to Make Folder Games 7

Flannel Board Numerals 8

Part One: Developing Number Concepts, One to Five

    Number One — "Hickory, Dickory, Dock" 9

    Number Two — "The Apple Tree" 24

    Number Three — "Three Wild Geese" 36

    Number Four — "Four Little Fishes" 47

    Number Five — "Five Little Monkeys" 57

Part Two: Developing Number Concepts, Six to Ten

    Number Six — "I Bought the Circus" 68

    Number Seven — "Going to St. Ives" 76

    Number Eight — "An Old Man with a Beard" 85

    Number Nine — "Nine Ponies" 95

    Number Ten — "Penguin Parade" 103

Part Three: Introducing Addition and Subtraction

    Addition — "Doubles" 114

    More Addition — "Adding One" 128

    Subtraction — "More Queen of Hearts" 134

Introduction

The purpose of *Whole Language Units for Math* is to make math more fun. Children learn number concepts and operations in connection with literature, games, and manipulative activities.

Every activity in this book has been tested in a real classroom. Even very young children can be exposed to rhyme, number, and play activities. Simply eliminate the more difficult activities and do not expect mastery. For kindergarteners, use this book as a supplement to the regular math text or use alone.

First graders can use *Whole Language Units for Math* at the beginning of the year as a review. More emphasis should be placed on the actual ability of the students to read the poems and related literature at this level. Make tapes and student copies of the poems to use at all levels.

An extensive sample plan is presented in "Hickory, Dickory, Dock" to assist the teacher in learning how to use the whole math method.

What Is Whole Math?

Whole math is fun. Emphasis is placed on reading books, participating in activities, and playing in centers. The natural work of children is play. Whole math stands in direct contrast to the "old way" of teaching math that consisted of a lecture followed by a workbook.

Whole math is introduced with a story or number rhyme. A Math Big Book is the ideal way to do this. Later in the lesson cycle, the teacher can read other books related to the topic. Each unit contains a model for a Math Big Book and related literature.

Whole math emphasizes manipulatives. Worksheets are used for practice and evaluation. Much of the daily schedule is spent in learning centers rather than lecture. It is essential to provide materials related to the literature selection for the children to use in centers. There should be a strong connection between the materials and the literature, and the connection should be emphasized.

Connecting statements are very important in whole math. Children do not automatically see the connection between counting mice and reciting "Hickory, Dickory, Dock." They have to learn to see relationships.

Some examples of connecting statements are:

> "The mouse may have been looking for some cheese when he ran up the clock. Let's play a game on the flannel board called Feed the Mice."

> "Since we are learning about 'Hickory, Dickory, Dock,' let's look at some clocks. Do you think a mouse can learn about numbers? No, he can't, but you can."

> "Clocks have numerals on them, like the clock in 'Hickory, Dickory, Dock.' The clock in our room has numerals. Let's take a walk outside and see if we can find some other numerals."

Repetition is essential to whole math. While repetition may be boring to teachers, children cannot learn without it. Number concepts are new to children. Cumulative repetition is especially effective. If the teacher teaches the number "one" for three days, a poem about "one" should be read each of the three days. After moving to the next number, the poem about the number "one" should be read whenever possible.

Presenting a Whole Math Unit

Each unit in this book includes a poem that relates to the number or math concept being studied. A reproducible Little Book of the poem for the children is also provided. Patterns that can be used to illustrate the poem while it is being recited are also included.

Choose a method to present the poem. Possibilities include a teacher-prepared Big Book, flannel board, magnetic board, chart, or transparencies. An easy method of presentation is to make transparencies of the Little Book pages.

Repeat the poem each day, varying the method of presentation. See suggestions in sample lessons. After presentation, students may follow along in their Little Books. Older children can actually learn to read the poem.

Copy a Little Book for each child. Play "find the word" games. Have children point to rhyming words or number words.

Do oral or written cloze activities. In cloze activities, leave a word out and ask the students to supply the missing word. For example: Hickory, Dickory, _____.

Encourage children to read Little Books to themselves or to a partner.

Repeat math concepts using flannel board manipulatives, games, and math manipulatives. It is extremely important to emphasize the connection between the poem or book and the following math activity. Demonstrate activities using flannel board and overhead. Then place them in centers as described below.

Extending the Unit

Math Center: Extend practice and understanding with math games. Use felt figures on the flannel board, folder games, or simply laminate the patterns to use as tabletop math games. Numeral cards (flash cards) can be made as quick color-and-cut figures, interfacing, or index cards. Use similar methods to make addition and subtraction problem cards. Encourage children to use their imaginations to act out the poems and make up stories for the flannel board characters. Include laminated copies of Little Book pages.

Science Center: Provide materials and displays for the children to manipulate. For example, provide live fish for "Four Little Fishes," or plastic or real foods to sort for "The Apple Tree." Include related library books about fish and fruits.

Block Center: Add plastic zoo animals for "Five Little Monkeys" and "I Bought the Circus." Stuffed animals can also be used.

Dramatic Play/House: Add puppets for any unit. Use patterns to make headbands of monkeys. Make crowns for royalty. Add appropriate clothing to use as costumes. Used stuffed animals to play circus.

Using the Patterns

For each of the poems in this book, patterns and props are provided. You can complete many activities if you seek help from students, aides, and volunteer parents. You do not have to use everything in this book. Begin by making copies of the Little Book pages for the students. If you are unable to find time to make any of the manipulatives, you can always copy some of the patterns on manila paper to make a teacher set. Manila paper will adhere slightly to a slanted flannel board. If you decide to color the patterns, students will enjoy helping. Use your imagination and adapt each activity to your own needs and talents. Any pattern can be shrunk or enlarged on a copier. Also keep in mind that manipulatives can take many forms: felt, colored index, transparencies, etc.

Traditional Felt Figures

Trace the patterns on felt squares, which can be purchased in craft, department, or fabric stores. Use very sharp scissors to cut. Attach pieces to each other using fabric or extra heavy tacky craft glue. Craft stores also have movable eyes and tiny pompoms to use for noses. Many activities require numerals on the figures. Write the numerals with a fine point permanent marker or write them on a small piece of tag and glue to the felt figures. Use felt figures to act out stories and math activities on the flannel board. If no flannel board is available for centers, children can place the felt figures directly on the carpet or on carpet squares. Make two sets of figures, one for the teacher and one for the children. Encourage children to make up their own stories and math problems.

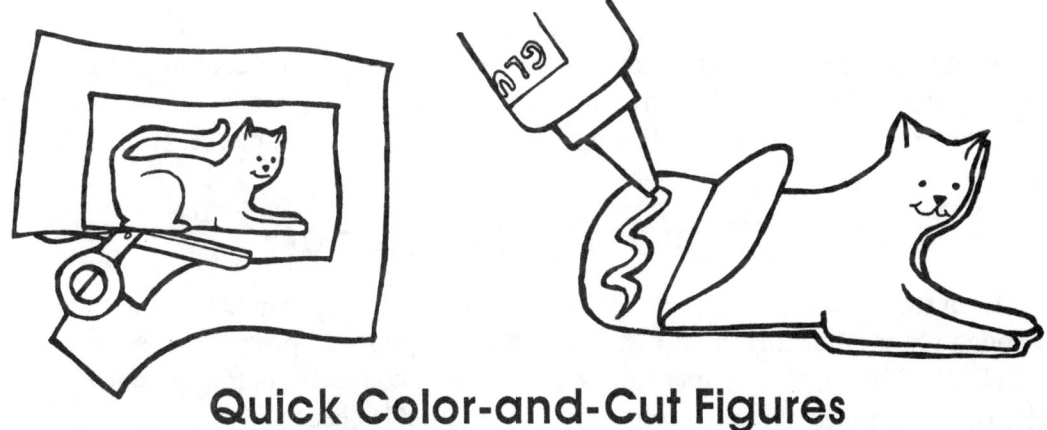

Quick Color-and-Cut Figures

Copy, color, and cut out the flannel board patterns. Many copiers will copy on heavy stock like index, tag, or construction paper. These papers can be purchased in many sizes, including the standard 8½" x 11" (22 cm x 28 cm). If colored papers are used, little or no coloring will be required. Patterns can also be copied on wallpaper samples cut to fit the copier. This eliminates coloring, because the resulting figures have a delightful 3-D appearance. Laminate. Glue felt to the back for flannel board use. Attach magnetic strips (available from office supply stores) for use on magnetic boards.

Fabric Interfacing Flannel Board Figures and Flash Cards

Put heavy non-woven interfacing (available in fabric stores) over the patterns and trace with a fine point permanent marker. (Pellon 930® works well.) Color with crayons. Numeral and equation cards can be made from interfacing also. Trace the patterns on page 8 to make numeral cards. These can be ironed if they become wrinkled.

Using the Patterns (cont.)

Puppets and Paper Dolls Math Games

Give each child copies of the patterns to color, cut out, and glue or tape to craft sticks for their own stick puppets. To make a teacher set, copy on heavy paper and laminate before taping to craft sticks. To make paper dolls, simply eliminate the craft sticks and place in a center. Most of the math activities may be adapted to three different forms: flannel board, folder game, or table top games. Use the paper doll method to make table top games of the math activities.

Bulletin Boards

Most of the chapters have related bulletin boards. To make very large pieces, place patterns on an opaque projector or enlarge on a copy machine. Using the banner maker on a computer is another easy way to make a title. To enlarge a poem to chart or bulletin board size, use a copier. You can also retype on computer software that has the ability to produce large typeface.

To Make a Big Book

Make a Big Book to present the poem, or for children to read in centers. Use a copy machine to enlarge the Little Book pages to 11" x 17" (28 cm x 43 cm). For a quicker method, do this on heavy colored paper. Glue to poster board and laminate. Making Big Books is a good activity for children. The teacher may pencil in the text for the children to trace with a water-based marker or let the children glue on strips or print prepared before the lesson. Children can color and glue on patterns from this book or draw their own illustrations. Let them outline their drawings with a black marker for a finished look.

Figures for Overhead

Figures made from felt or paper can sometimes be used directly on the overhead if their outlines are distinctive enough for easy identification. The easiest way to present a poem is to use transparencies made from the Little Book pages. If time allows, these can be colored with transparency pens. Make transparencies of the activity pages also, when extra instruction is needed.

To Assemble Little Books

Have copies of the Little Book pages made for each child. Cut along dotted lines. During class, have the students color the pages. Show them how to put the pages in order. Add one or two blank pages at the end for them to add their own ideas or for the practice of words and numerals. Staple completed books. Students follow along in their Little Books during repeated readings of the poems and then take them home to share.

Student-Made Books and Math Projects

You can use any of the patterns or numerals for students to create their own math projects or number books. Provide copies of patterns and large paper or a booklet on which to glue them.

How To Make Folder Games

Children can make their own folder games to take home and share with parents. This provides valuable additional practice for math skills. The teacher can prepare a sample folder ahead of time to use as a visual aid. Many of the games described as flannel board games can also be prepared as folder games. For the sake of simplicity, the folder game from "The Apple Tree" is described here. The steps are similar for most folder games.

The students can use discarded file folders to make their games. If no discarded folders are available, use large sheets of manila paper or 12" x 18" (30 cm x 46 cm) construction paper. Work with four or five students at a time. Center time is best.

1. The students use templates or patterns provided on page 31 to make five large apples from red paper. Wide-mouth plastic glasses can be used for templates. The teacher may wish to precut the apples for very young children.

2. Assist the children as they glue apples inside the folder. Be careful to put the glue on the backs of the apples in a U shape. Emphasize the importance of leaving the open part of the U at the top of the apple. Let dry overnight.

3. Copy page 32 on heavy green paper or green wallpaper. Have students cut out the worms.

4. If you wish, glue an answer sheet to the back of the folder. Encourage students to use their games at home.

5. Students can decorate the front of the folder with the art project described on page 27 or design their own cover art.

6. Demonstrate how to count the holes and match the numeral on the worm to the apple. The worm slides behind the apple so that it looks like it is living in the apple.

Flannel Board Numerals

Make a set of numerals for a flannel board. See page 5 for directions. These numerals can also be used for various activities throughout this book, or students may simply cut out and glue them in order.

#200 Whole Language Units for Math — 8 — ©1993 Teacher Created Materials, Inc.

Hickory, Dickory, Dock

Hickory, dickory, dock!

The mouse ran up the clock;

The clock struck one,

The mouse ran down,

Hickory, dickory, dock!

Hickory, Dickory, Dock

Sample Lessons

Day 1: Make an interactive clock bulletin board. Make three copies of the clock on page 22 and draw in hands for 1, 2, and 3 o'clock. Glue clock faces to large rectangular pieces of colored paper so that they look like grandfather clocks. Use a computer or a copy machine to enlarge the text of "Hickory, Dickory, Dock" and place it on the bulletin board near the clocks. Prepare and laminate small numeral cards for 1, 2, and 3 using 3" x 5" (8 cm x 13 cm) index cards. Place three strawberry baskets on or under the clocks to hold numeral cards. Make a title for the bulletin board using a computer banner maker: Hickory, Dickory, Dock. Use the mouse and cat patterns on pages 17-18.

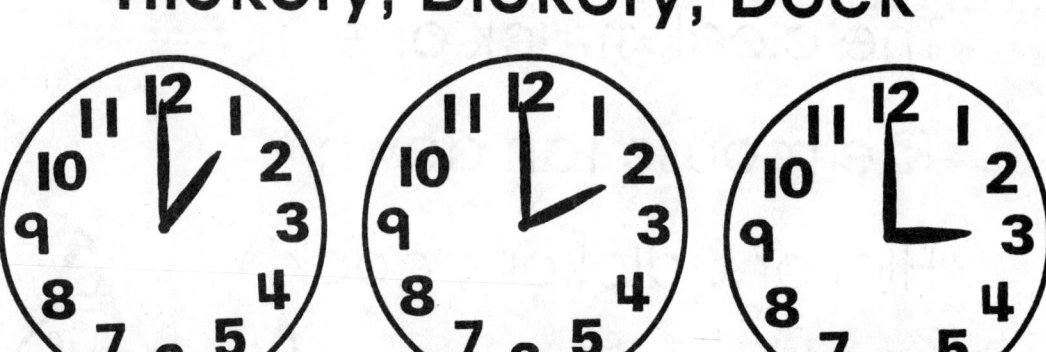

Introduce "Hickory, Dickory, Dock." Call the children's attention to the bulletin board. Point to the title and ask if anyone can guess what the words say. Read the nursery rhyme aloud using a pointer to indicate each word. Ask if anyone knows why the mouse ran up the clock. Tell them that perhaps he wanted to learn about numbers and clocks. Explain the time on each of the clocks.

Instruct the children to look at the little hand only. Model the matching activity by placing each numeral card in the basket under the appropriate clock. For example, the numeral 1 card should be placed under the clock that shows 1 o'clock. Let students interact with the bulletin board each day by placing the numeral cards in the strawberry baskets. After a few days replace numeral cards with three Mouse Match Cards to sustain interest. The Mouse Match Card pattern is on page 19. Enlarge them slightly for this activity.

Play Counting on Cheese. Use yellow or orange felt to prepare as many pieces of cheese as you need from the pattern on page 16. Cut holes by folding felt and cutting out small circular sections. Cut one hole in the first piece, two holes in second piece, three holes in the third piece, etc. Place the pieces of cheese on the flannel board in random order. Let the students pretend to be mice. A mouse can get a piece of cheese by correctly counting the number of holes. Assist students so they can place the pieces back on the flannel board in counting order by counting the holes.

Hickory, Dickory, Dock

Sample Lessons *(cont.)*

In the math center have children do some free exploration. Let them use a flannel board and manipulatives. Materials to use include: felt cheese (page 16), felt shapes of different sizes and colors, felt or interfacing mice and cats (page 17), interfacing clock faces set to different times (page 22), and felt numerals or small numeral cards on index with felt backs (page 8).

Day 2: Repeat the poem each day by reading a Big Book, chart, or transparency of "Hickory, Dickory, Dock." If you have a tape or record which features this poem, use it and listen to some other nursery rhymes as well. Continue with other counting records. One that never seems to grow old is Hap Palmer's *Math Readiness Album*.

Do one-to-one matching. Place five mice far apart on the left side of the flannel board. On the right side, place the five pieces of felt cheese close together. Ask: "Are there enough pieces of cheese to feed all these mice?" Take predictions. Rearrange the cheese so that the pieces are spaced like the mice. Then use pieces of yarn to draw lines from each mouse to each piece of cheese. Explain one-to-one matching and the concept of same number.

Prepare Mouse Match cards to use in the math center. Use the Quick Color-and-Cut Figure method. Patterns are on page 19. Make Set I on one color of tag and Set II on another color. Tell the students to match the cards that have the same number.

Create a special math center for a simple domino game. Divide the dominoes equally between players. Start the game with a double. Instruct the students that the same number must touch the same number. The dominoes in each player's hand are displayed face up. The player may choose any domino in his/her hand to play. Play continues until all possible dominoes have been played.

Day 3: Reread "Hickory, Dickory, Dock" using the Little Book transparencies. Follow up by reading *The Completed Hickory Dickory Dock* by Jim Aylesworth (Atheneum, 1990). This book is so much fun the students won't realize how much they are learning.

Duplicate the Mouse Catcher worksheet on page 21 for each student. Before completing the worksheet draw a similar exercise on the chalkboard using mice and blueberries (circles). Let students draw lines to match mice to circles.

Play a story. Prepare flannel board figures to allow the children to play "Hickory, Dickory, Dock" and *The Completed Hickory Dickory Dock*. You will need clocks, mice, cats, bees, blueberries, and a book. See pages 17 and 18 for patterns.

Place the pattern pieces from *The Completed Hickory Dickory Dock* in the library or math center, along with the book. Tell the children to play the story or make up a new story.

Hickory, Dickory, Dock

Sample Lessons (cont.)

Let children do some gluing in the fine motor center. Place copies of page 23 along with glue and dried beans in a center. Students glue beans to the numeral 1. Explain and demonstrate this activity to the whole class before going to centers or drop by the center later to offer individualized help.

Day 4: Reread "Hickory, Dickory, Dock." Let the children slap their legs in rhythm while singing "Hickory, Dickory, Dock." Explain that there are other nursery rhymes about numbers. Share "Little Jumping Joan" and have the children guess what number goes with the rhyme. Follow up with individual jump ropes outside.

Little Jumping Joan

Here am I,

Little Jumping Joan,

When nobody's with me

I'm always alone.

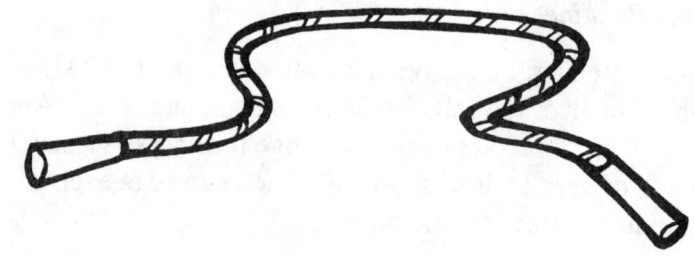

Help the mouse find the cheese. Ask the children to help the mouse by tracing the path in the maze on page 20. They may use fingers, crayons, or pencils. If children have never done a maze, you may wish to make a transparency to demonstrate.

Place a toy clock and a rubber mouse in the block center. (Rubber mice can often be purchased in the cat toy section of grocery stores or pet stores.) Challenge the children to build a block maze for the mouse to find the clock.

If you have cat and mouse puppets, use them in the dramatic play center along with a toy clock and a copy of "Hickory, Dickory, Dock" or *The Completed Hickory Dickory Dock*.

Day 5: Give a child an opportunity to read the poem. Then read the book *Mice Twice* by Joseph Low (Aladdin, 1986). Explain that "twice" means two times and that tomorrow children will be learning about the number two.

Have children put the clocks in order. Prepare interfacing clocks or cut-and-color clocks for the flannel board. Patterns are on page 16. Then have them put the felt pieces of cheese in order by the number of holes again. Use numeral cards to match the clocks and the number of holes in the cheese.

Cheese, please! Cut yellow construction paper in half. Show students how to cut straight lines diagonally to make about five pieces of cheese. Use a black crayon to make holes in the cheese. Display the felt pieces of cheese on the flannel board for the children to copy.

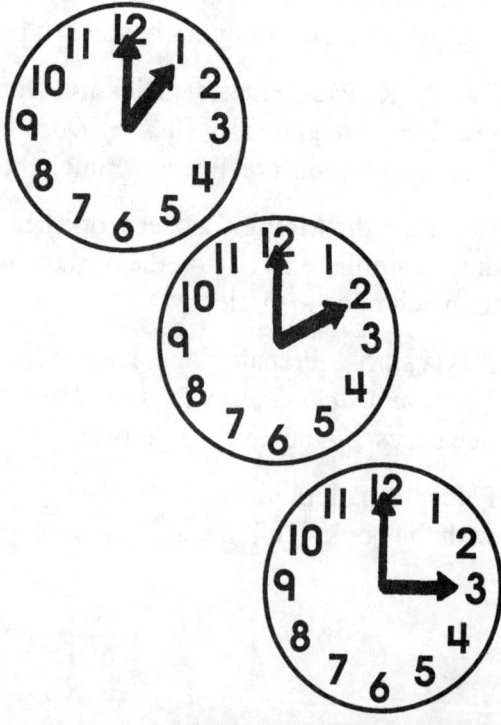

Place the clocks, cheese, and numeral cards in the math center so that the students can practice counting order activities.

Little Book

My Little Book of
Hickory, Dickory, Dock

Name _____

Hickory, dickory, dock!

1

Hickory, Dickory, Dock

Little Book (cont.)

The mouse ran up the clock;

2

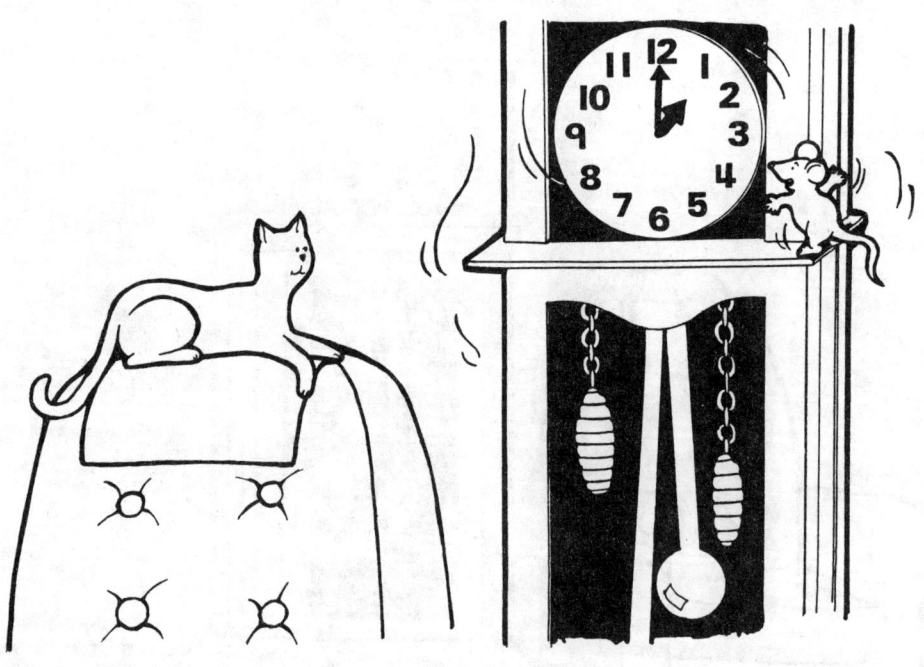

The clock struck one,

3

Little Book (cont.)

The mouse ran down,

Hickory, dickory, dock!

Hickory, Dickory, Dock

Patterns

Make five pieces of cheese. Make one with one hole, one with two holes, etc.

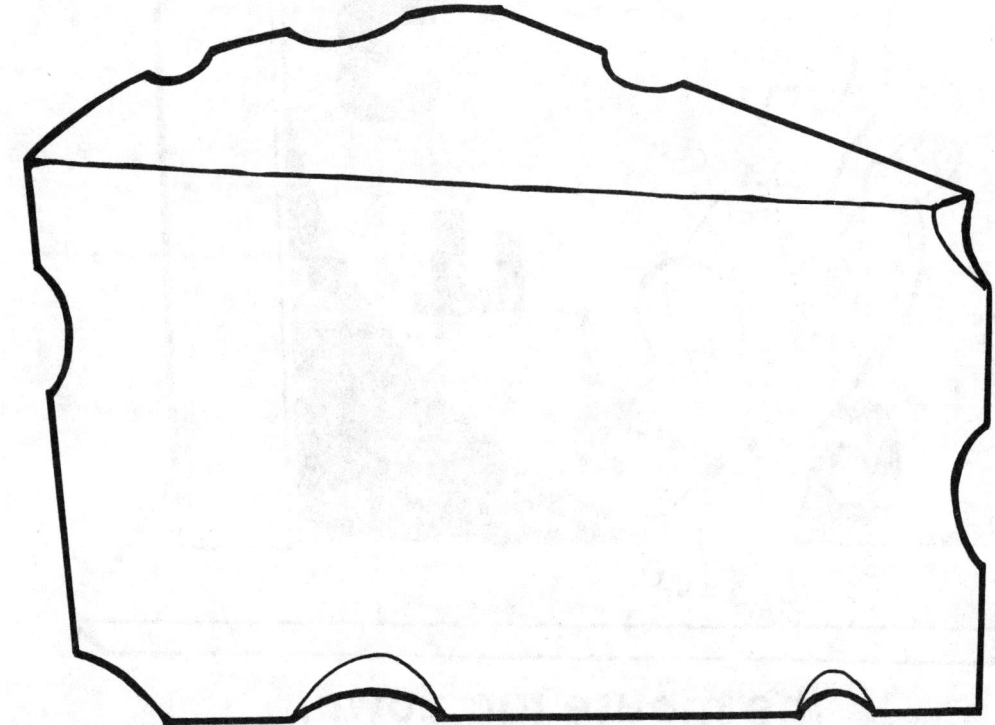

Make five clock faces showing the hours from 1 o'clock to 5 o'clock.

#200 Whole Language Units for Math ©1993 Teacher Created Materials, Inc.

Hickory, Dickory, Dock

Patterns *(cont.)*

©1993 Teacher Created Materials, Inc. #200 Whole Language Units for Math

Hickory, Dickory, Dock

Patterns (cont.)

#200 Whole Language Units for Math   ©1993 Teacher Created Materials, Inc.

Hickory, Dickory, Dock

Mouse Match Cards

Make 2 sets on different colored index. Laminate. Glue to felt.

Hickory, Dickory, Dock

Name _____

Help the Mouse Find the Cheese!

There is only one way to the cheese.

Hickory, Dickory, Dock

Name _____

Mouse Catchers

If every cat catches a mouse, will any mice get away? Draw lines to match each cat to a mouse.

Hickory, Dickory, Dock
Bulletin Board Clock Pattern
Draw hands or attach hands. See directions on page 10.

#200 Whole Language Units for Math ©1993 Teacher Created Materials, Inc.

Hickory, Dickory, Dock

Name _____

Number 1

Directions: Glue beans to the large 1. Color the mouse and clock.

The Apple Tree

Away up high in the apple tree,

Two red apples smiled at me.

I shook that tree as hard as I could;

Down came those apples,

And mmmm, they were good!

The Apple Tree

Sample Lessons

Day 1: Make an apple bulletin board. Make an apple tree by drawing a large cloud shape on green bulletin board paper. Add a trunk by drawing a rectangular shape on brown bulletin board paper.

Cut apples from red construction paper or tag. Begin by placing two apples on the tree. Ask children to count the apples. The number of apples on the tree can be changed daily or weekly, as you wish, to provide counting practice for your class after opening exercises. After counting, tack the correct numeral on the tree. Add more trees if you have room.

Body math is an easy way to count. Choose a child to stand in front of the room to be a model. Ask some of the following questions: How many eyes do you have? How many heads do you have? How many ears do you have? How many hands do you have? How many feet do you have? How many noses do you have? How many nostrils do you have? How many necks do you have? How many cheeks do you have? How many eyebrows do you have?

Pose this challenge. How many fingers do you have? How many toes do you have? Can you guess how many hairs are on your head?

Repeat these questions each day until children can answer quickly and easily.

As a follow-up, tell the children that since they have learned how many face parts they have, they are to look at a neighbor and draw his/her face. Remind them to draw the correct number of ears, nostrils, and eyebrows.

Make worms and apples. Use the patterns on page 31 to make five large felt apples and the patterns on page 32 to make fifteen green felt worms. Cut worm holes in the apples by folding and cutting with scissors. Give each apple a different number of holes (one-five). Show the class how to place the apples in order by counting the holes. Place the felt apples and worms in a math center.

The Apple Tree

Sample Lessons (cont.)

Day 2: Present the poem. Use the flannel board or a Big Book to present the poem. Read the poem a second time and leave out key words for the children to guess (cloze).

Change the number of apples on the flannel board and let the children count them. Repeat the first two lines of the poem and change the number. For example:

Away up high in the apple tree,

Four red apples smiled at me.

Distribute Little Books (pages 28-30). Have students color and assemble them to share at home.

Make five apple trees out of light green felt. The pattern is on page 33. Write a numeral (1-5) on each with a permanent fine point marker. Cut fifteen apples from the pattern on page 33 or use red circles. Place the trees and circles in the math center so that the children can read the numeral and put the correct number of apples on each tree.

Day 3: Reread the poem. Ask the children to brainstorm some things that always come in twos. (Some examples include socks, shoes, gloves, and mittens.) Explain that another word for "two" is "pair." Use the word in a few sentences to illustrate its use. "I am wearing a pair of gloves. You are wearing a pair of socks." Another word that means "two" is "couple." "Hansel and Gretel are a couple. Jack and Jill are a couple. If I ask one of you to bring me a couple of crayons, you will bring me two crayons." (Refer to TCM 020 *Whole Language Units for Nursery Rhymes*, for a unit on "Jack and Jill" that can be used as related learning.) Emphasize the number two throughout.

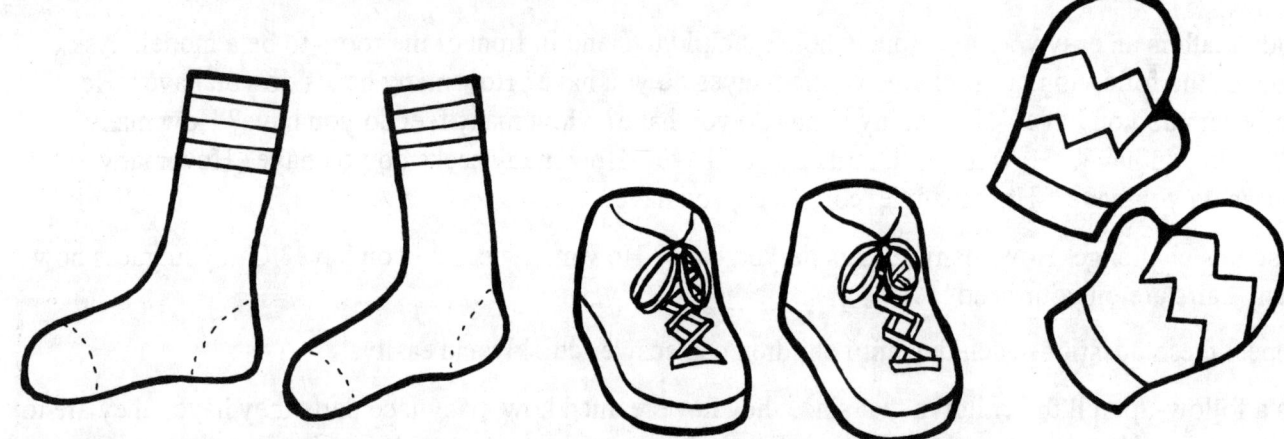

Go outside to practice skipping. After some practice, have the children hold hands and skip as couples. Emphasize that couple means two.

Have children make "corny" twos. Set up a special math center with bowls of unpopped popcorn kernels and glue. Distribute a copy of page 34 for each child. Students glue popcorn on the numeral and color the apples. Connect corn with apples by pointing out that both grow on plants. As an extension, talk about fruits and vegetables as you work.

The Apple Tree

Sample Lessons *(cont.)*

Day 4: Act out the poem using real or paper apples. Then teach a counting rhyme, "Hot Cross Buns." Use the pattern on page 32 for hot cross buns.

Hot Cross Buns

Hot cross buns! Hot cross buns!

One a penny, two a penny,

Hot cross buns!

Explain that hot cross buns are round bread or rolls. The cross is a design on the bun. Children will understand about peddlers if you have read *Caps for Sale*. Let two children sing a duet pretending to be the peddlers.

Prepare a folder game as shown. Demonstrate how to play the folder game. Then let children make their own folder games in centers. Work with small groups of students to help them. Display the finished game as a guide. You will need construction paper, scissors, glue, crayons, and a black watercolor marker. Students can use discarded folders or fold a large sheet of manila paper for a folder. Tips for making folder games are on page 7.

Day 5: Some students may be able to read the poem for the class by now. Let these students teach the poem using a pointer. Allow quiet time for independent reading practice with the Little Books.

Distribute the worm maze on page 35. Explain that two worms were looking for an apple tree. They went different ways to look for the tree and they both found the same tree. There are two correct paths to the tree. Children can use two different-colored crayons to indicate the two different paths.

Have children work at the art center on this activity. Students paint or draw trees. Provide red construction paper for the children to cut apples freehand. An easy way to make circles is to cut a square and then trim the corners. Students may glue as many apples on the tree as they wish. Tell them to count the apples and write the correct numeral somewhere on the paper. The teacher may need to write the numeral for younger children.

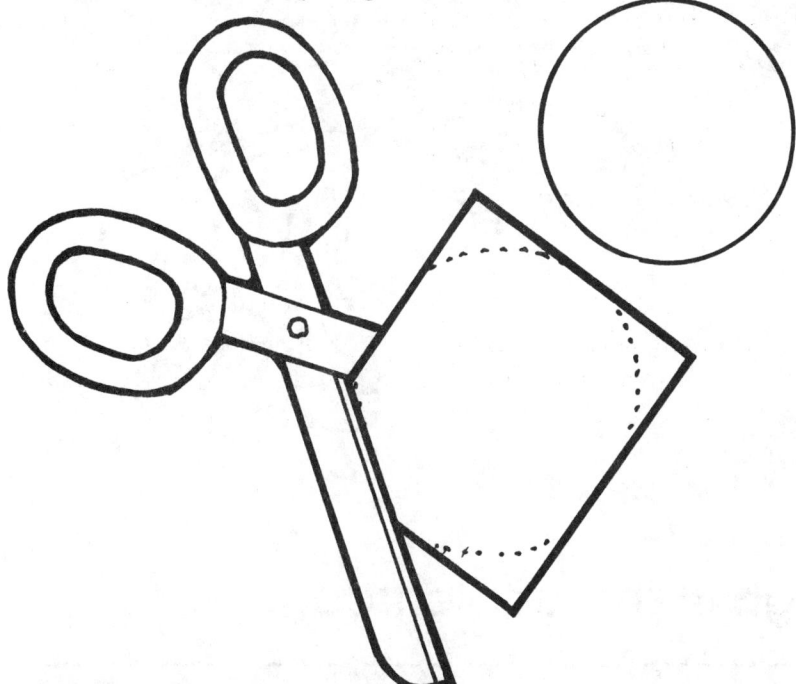

©1993 Teacher Created Materials, Inc.   #200 *Whole Language Units for Math*

The Apple Tree

Little Book

My Little Book of
The Apple Tree

Name: _____

Away up high in the apple tree,

1

The Apple Tree

Little Book (cont.)

Two red apples smiled at me.

2

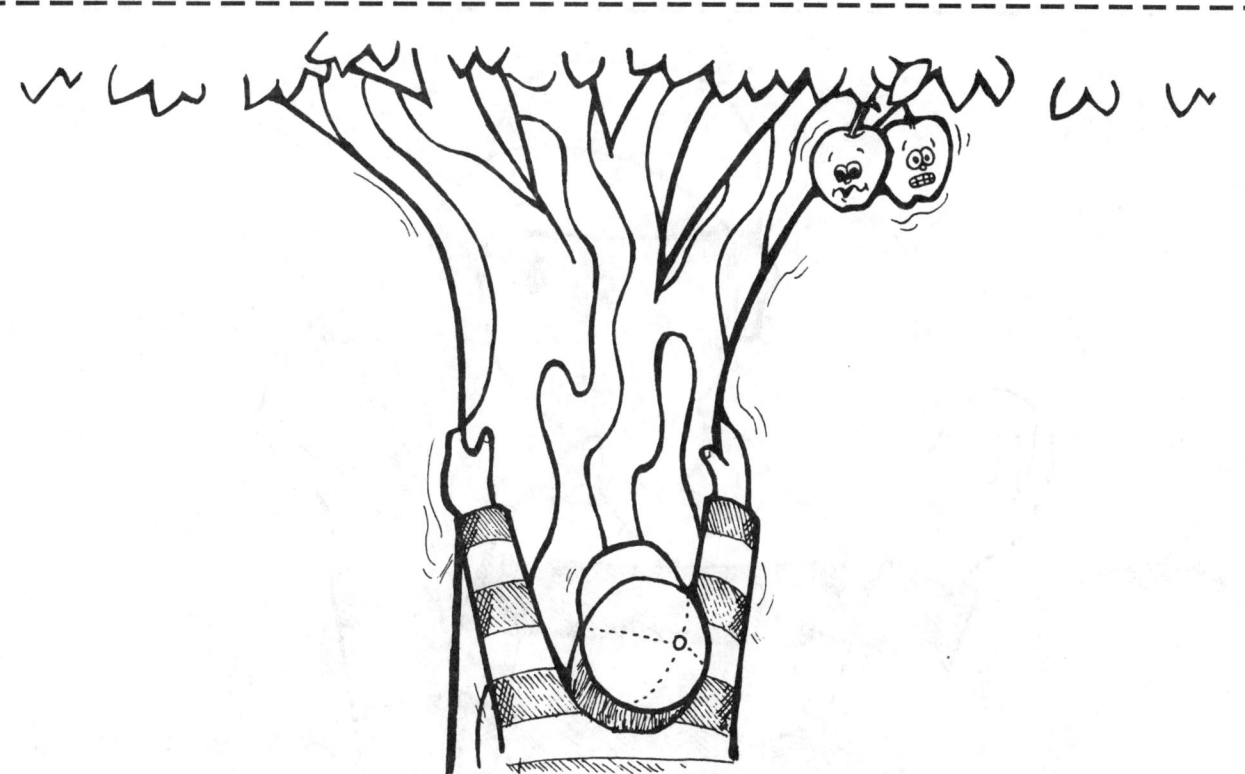

I shook that tree as hard as I could;

3

The Apple Tree

Little Book (cont.)

Down came those apples,

4

And mmmm, they were good!

5

The Apple Tree

Patterns

The Apple Tree

Patterns (cont.)

Use these worms for the folder game. Copy them onto heavy paper.

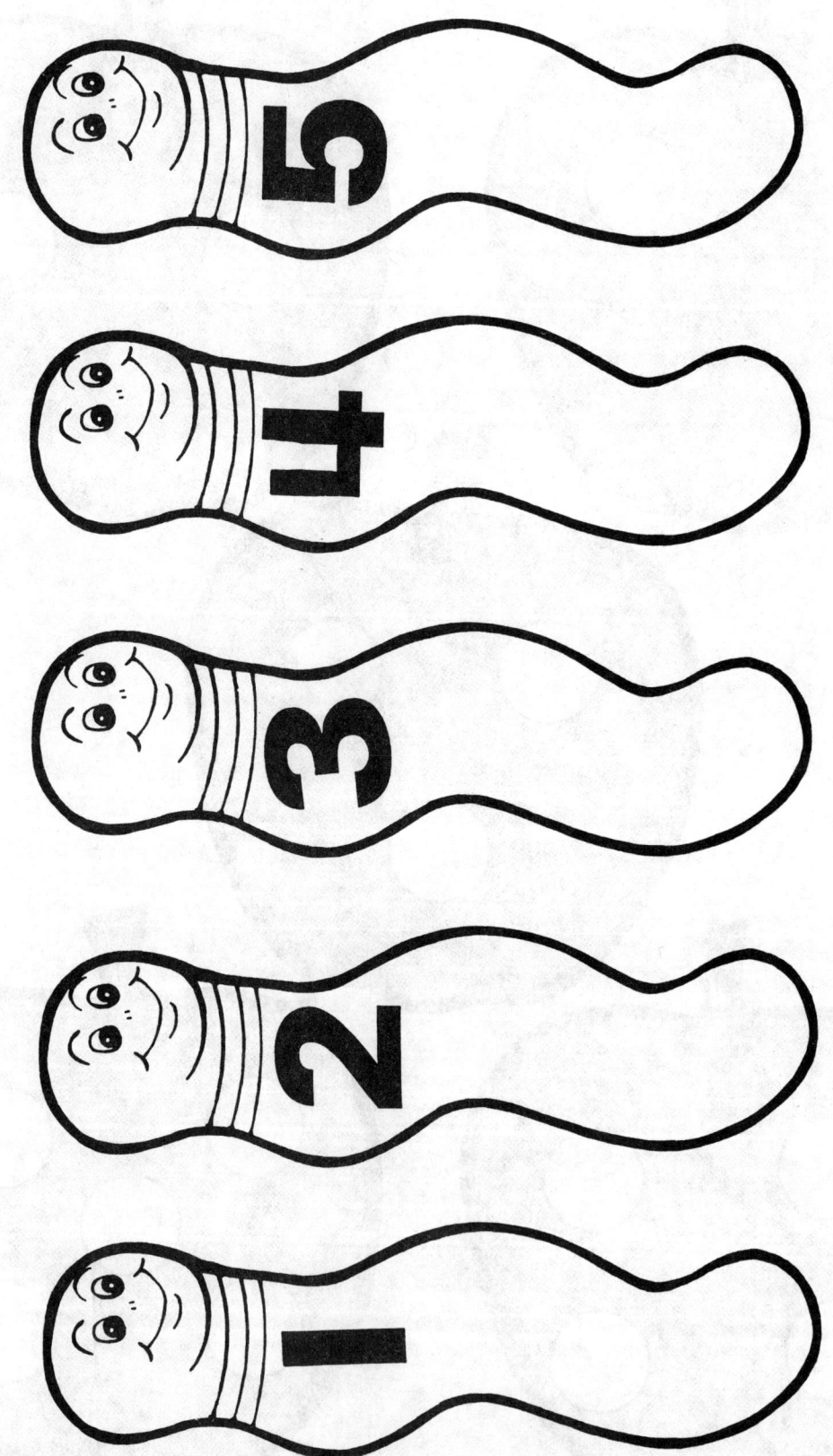

#200 Whole Language Units for Math 32 ©1993 Teacher Created Materials, Inc.

The Apple Tree

Patterns *(cont.)*

The Apple Tree

Name _____

Number 2

Directions: Glue unpopped popcorn kernels to the 2. Color the apples.

The Apple Tree

Name _____

Two Ways to the Apple Tree

There are two ways to the apple tree. Can you find them both?

©1993 Teacher Created Materials, Inc.

Three Wild Geese

Intery, mintery, cutery corn,

Apple seed and apple thorn;

Wire, brier, limber-lock,

Three wild geese in a flock.

One flew east, one flew west,

And one flew over the cuckoo's nest.

Three Wild Geese

Sample Plans

Day 1: Create a bulletin board similar to the illustration below. (Use the patterns on page 42.) Include a copy of the poem on page 36. Copy it onto chart paper or enlarge on a computer.

Play Geese in a Flock at a flannel board. Make geese from white felt or interfacing. Use a permanent fine point marker to write numerals 1-5 on the geese. Patterns can be found on page 42. Place the geese on the flannel board. Identify the numerals on each goose. Ask the children: How many geese are on the flannel board? (5) Which is more: 5 or 3? (5)

Place the geese in numerical order and explain counting order. Then mix up the geese. Give children a chance to place the geese in counting order when they visit the math center.

(It is helpful to explain that wild birds are usually dark colors such as gray or black, but that most white geese live on a farm. Also explain the difference between ducks and geese.)

All birds lay eggs. Ask the children where they have seen eggs. Geese, chickens, penguins, and all other birds lay eggs. Play a counting game with eggs and geese. Use the numeral geese from Geese in a Flock. Make fifteen interfacing or felt eggs. How many eggs will the #1 goose lay? She will lay 1 egg. Let a student read the numeral on the second goose and put the correct number of eggs (2) near the feet of the goose. Call on other students to read the numbers 3, 4, and 5 and then place the correct number of eggs on the flannel board. See bulletin board illustration.

Day 2: Introduce the Big Book. Invite the children to look at the cover art and guess what the book is about. Read through quickly for fun. Lead the children to connect the poem with the number three. Ask if the students know any other stories or poems about three. Allow them to recite or sing to the class.

Talk about geese and other birds. Read *Have You Seen Birds?* by Joanne Oppenheim (Scholastic, 1986).

Prepare the Little Books on pages 39-41 following directions on page 6. Little Books may be assembled by the teacher or the students. While most children will want to color the pages, it is not necessary for younger students. Keep the Little Books in the classroom while studying about the number 3. Add a blank page or two to the back of the Little Books for students to add their own ideas or to practice writing numerals.

Tearing construction paper is good for hand-eye coordination. Work with small groups in the art center until they produce a small pile of multi-colored confetti. Copy page 45 for each child. Instruct students to put a tiny amount of glue on part of the numeral 3 and then cover with tiny pieces of paper. Continue until the 3 is covered.

Three Wild Geese

Sample Lessons (cont.)

Day 3: Reread "Three Wild Geese" with the students following along in their Little Books. Ask questions: Can you find the word "geese?" What letter does it begin with? Three can be written as a word or as a numeral. Can you find the word "three" in your book? If children have difficulty, write "geese" and "three" on the chalkboard. Continue with similar questions.

Take a number walk to find numerals around the school inside and out. Look for some of the following: room numbers, telephones, computers, car license plates, house numbers, or scales. This might be a good time for the nurse to weigh and measure each child for school records.

Make nests and eggs. Discuss the term "oval" before beginning. Give each child an 8½" x 11" (22 cm x 28 cm) piece of brown paper. Cut off corners to make a large oval. Then cover the paper by writing the letter "x" many times with a black crayon to resemble sticks and straw. Have the children cut out three oval eggs from a piece of manila paper or white paper. Then glue the three eggs in the center of the brown paper nest.

Day 4: Reread the poem, pausing at key words for students to fill in missing words (oral cloze). Make a connecting statement by reminding the class that they are still learning about three. Then read any version of the "Three Little Kittens."

Make a simple Big Book. Fold a long sheet of colored bulletin board paper or brown craft paper in half lengthwise. Attach to a chalkboard, wall, or bulletin board with tape or tacks. Mark off page segments with a water-based black marker. Using the same marker, write "Book of 3" on the first page (cover). On each page write a large numeral 3. Students can participate by thinking about three. Under each 3, teacher or students can draw and paint three objects such as three eggs, birds, kittens, or flowers. Older students can write or trace words or sentences: "I see 3 eggs." Take down the paper and fold it in accordion fashion so that it makes a book. Staple and then tape the spine.

As a whole class activity or in centers have students make their own little "Book of 3." Give each child a piece of white paper and have them fold it twice. Cut on folds and the result will be four pages. The teacher can staple the four pages to make a book. Students should decide what objects they wish to draw to make a book similar to the Big Book made by the teacher. For younger students, the teacher or an aide can pencil in the numerals and the students can trace the 3's.

For homework give each child a heavy sheet of paper such as manila or tag. Glue page 43 on the front of the paper and page 44 on the back side. Cut into flash cards when dry and have children take home to practice.

Little Book

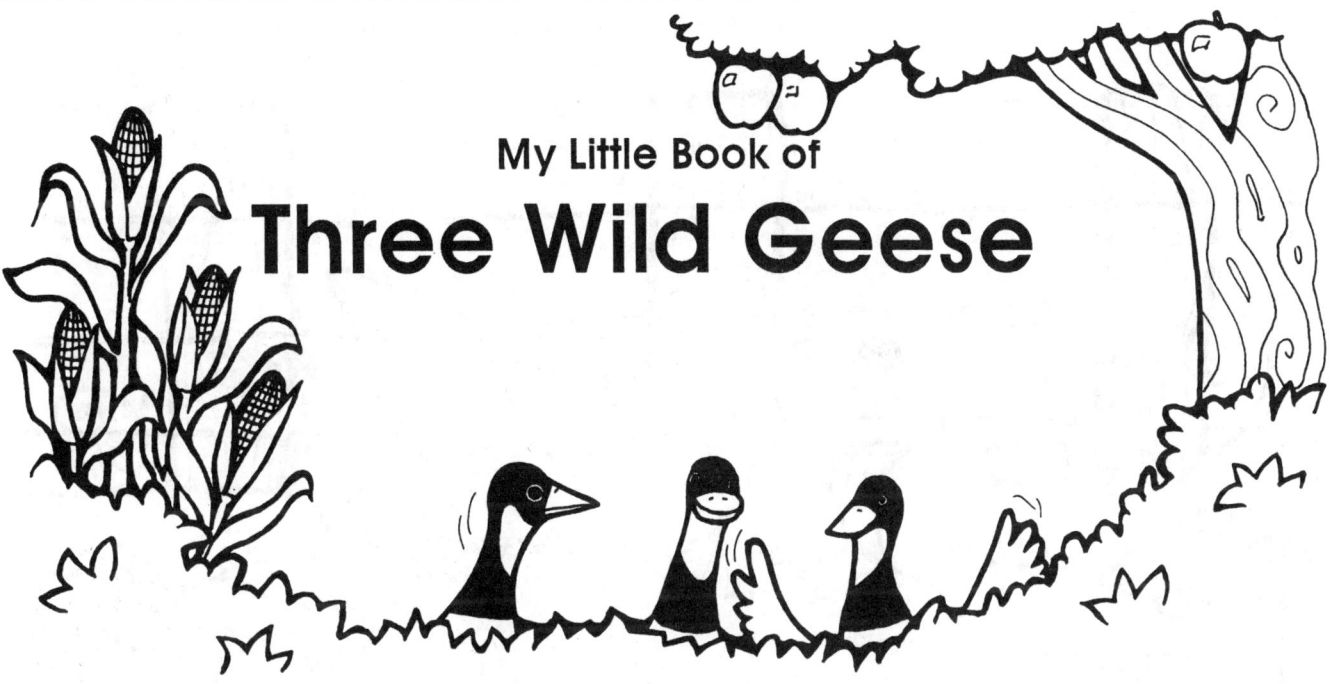

My Little Book of
Three Wild Geese

Name _____

Intery, mintery, cutery corn,
Apple seed and apple thorn;

1

Three Wild Geese

Little Book (cont.)

Wire, brier, limber-lock,
Three wild geese in a flock.

2

One flew east, one flew west,

3

Three Wild Geese

Little Book (cont.)

And one flew over the cuckoo's nest.

4

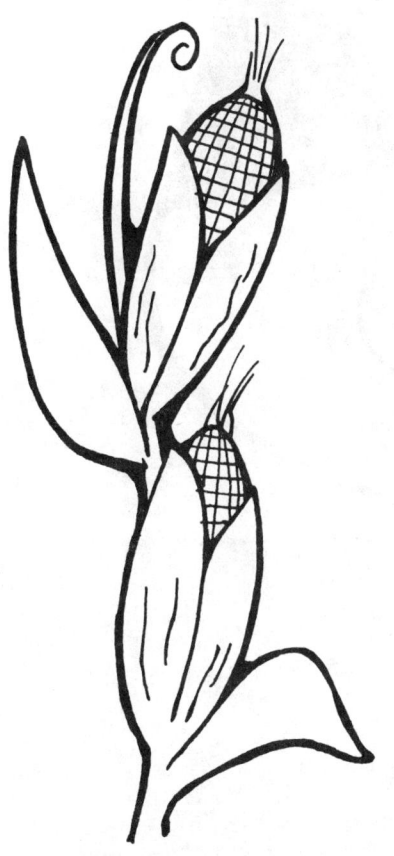

Show what you know.

5

Three Wild Geese

Patterns

#200 Whole Language Units for Math ©1993 Teacher Created Materials, Inc.

Three Wild Geese

Flash Cards

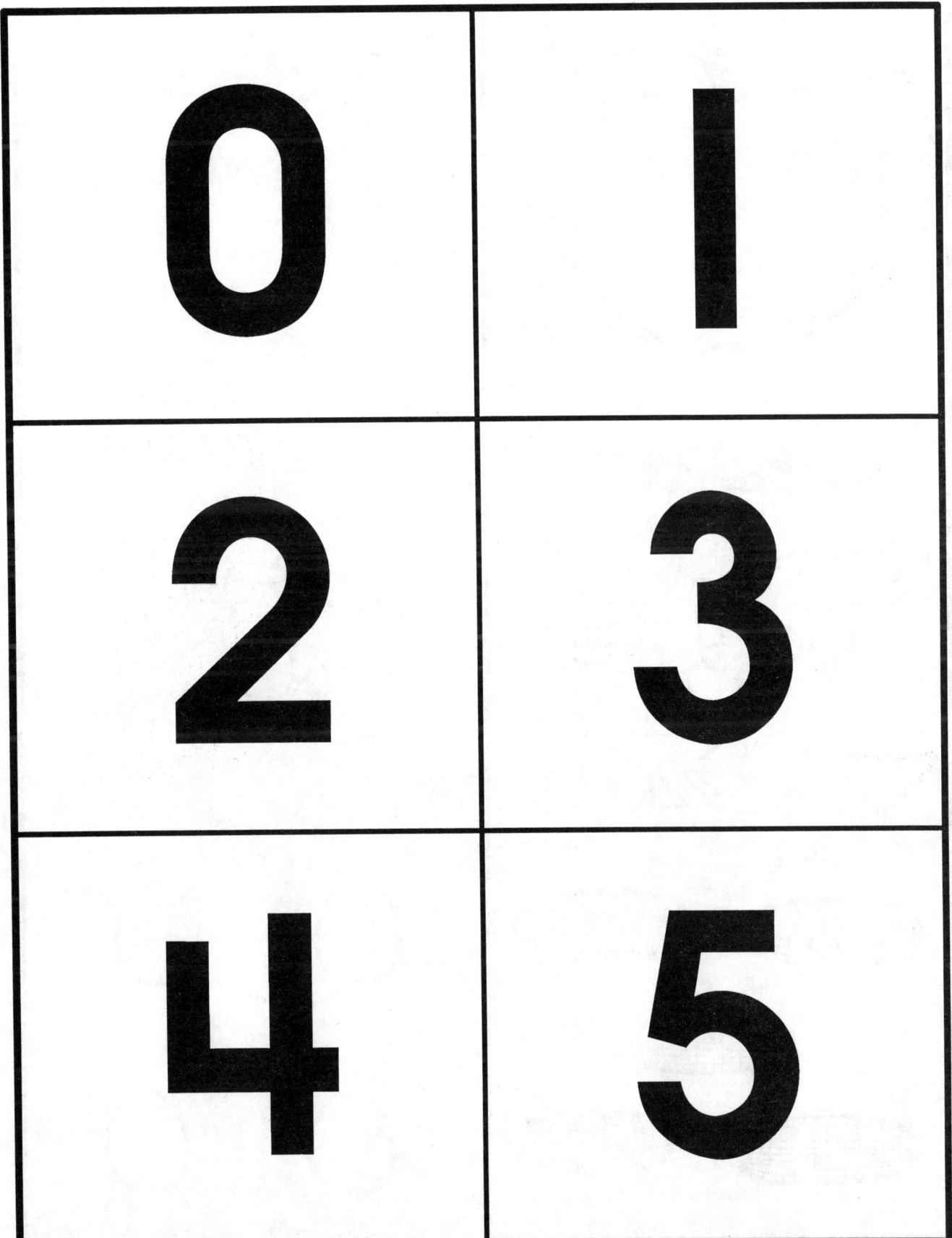

Three Wild Geese

Flash Cards *(cont.)*

Three Wild Geese

Name:_____

Number 3

Directions: Glue torn paper to the 3. Color the geese.

Three Wild Geese

Name:_____

Geese and Eggs

Each goose wants to sit on an egg. Will they each get one egg? Draw lines to find out.

#200 Whole Language Units for Math   ©1993 Teacher Created Materials, Inc.

Four Little Fishes

Four little fishes
Swimming in the sea.
Caught in a net,
They can't get free.
Out jumped the first
With a flip of his tail.
The second one shouted,
"I can jump like a whale."
The third one called,
"I'm coming too."
The fourth one yelled,
"I can jump like you."
Four little fishes
Swimming in the sea,
Singing all together,
"We're free! We're free!"

by Sandra Merrick

Four Little Fishes

Sample Plans

Day 1: Make a fish bulletin board. Cover the entire bulletin board with blue paper. After hearing the poem and looking at fish books, students can draw fish on colored paper using crayons or paint, cut out, and glue to the blue paper. (See the section below on how to create fish drawings.) This is an extremely easy and attractive board. Keep adding fish each day until the board is very full. It is fun to count the fish each day and pin up a card with the correct number. Title the board "Fish."

Introduce the poem by talking about fish. Where do fish live? What do they look like? Where have you seen fish? Read the poem from a chart or Big Book.

Bring in live fish. Minnows or goldfish will provide a lively discussion. Tell children all fish have scales. Most fish breathe oxygen from water using gills. Compare people to fish and talk about what would happen if they changed places. Place the fish in a special art center for a few days so that students can observe them while creating fish art.

Create fish drawings with crayons and colored paper. Provide reference books with many different kinds of fish. Give each student blue construction paper and a large plastic lid. Trace around the lid to make a bowl. Cut out the colorful fish drawings and glue on the bowl. See fish drawing lesson on page 54. Write the number of fish somewhere on the bowl. Younger children may need help with cutting, and the number may need to be traced rather than written. Draw an extra fish for the bulletin board.

Day 2: Recite the poem while placing felt fish on the flannel board. Act out the poem with the flannel board fish. Then read the book *Fish Eyes* by Lois Ehlert (HBJ, 1990).

Copy and assemble Little Books. Read the poem together and color the books. Add extra blank pages for students to add their own drawings or words. Let children keep them in desks for a few days.

Make a fishy math center. Use the patterns on page 53 to make four or five bowls from light blue felt. Write numerals on the bowls with a fine point permanent marker. Demonstrate how to place the bowls in counting order. Make small felt fish for students to place in each bowl. Place in math center with flannel board.

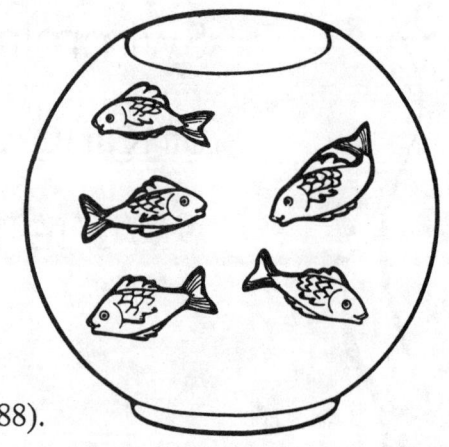

Day 3: Reread the poem using transparencies made from the Little Book on pages 50-52. Talk about fish food. Worms and insects are fish favorites. Fish food is called bait when it is used to catch fish. Follow up with a fun book, *How Many Bugs in a Box?* by David Carter (Simon & Schuster, 1988).

Four Little Fishes

Sample Lessons (cont.)

Match fish to worms on the flannel board. Explore situations with more fish, less fish, and the same number of fish and worms. Always take predictions from students before matching worms to fish.

Teach students an easy card game. Two players may play. Shuffle and deal the cards. Each player keeps his/her cards face down. Both players turn over the top card. The card with the greater number takes both cards. If both cards have the same number, each player retains his/her own card. After all cards have been played, the player with more cards is the winner.

Make cards for each student to take home. Make a master copy by dividing a sheet of paper into 12 squares. Leave two squares blank. In the next two squares place one dot each, in the next two squares two dots each, and so on up through the number 5. Reproduce onto index paper. Cut out and give each child a set. If no index paper is available, have students cut and glue cards onto manila paper. Cards can also be made by drawing dots onto index cards.

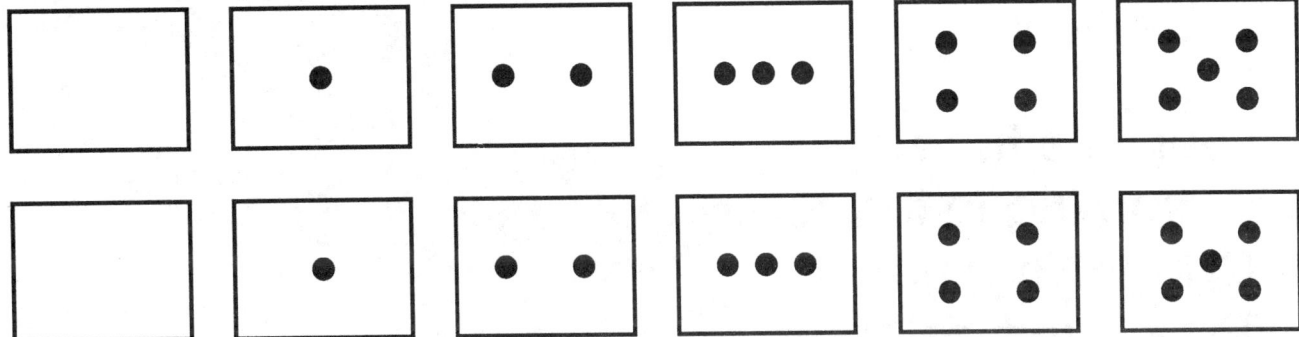

Day 4: Put your class in action as you reread the poem. Have the whole class jump every time a fish jumps out of the net. Then read a beautiful book, *Sea Squares*, by Joyce N. Hulme (Hyperion, 1991). This book can be made simpler on the first reading by leaving out the "squared" part and just concentrating on numbers 1 through 10. Place the book in the math center or in the class library.

Make a fish book. Demonstrate how to make a counting book using fish. Write or glue a numeral on four sheets of paper. Children draw the correct number of fish on each sheet. The teacher can staple each book once or twice to make student counting booklets.

Have a fishy art center. Cut out two large fish from heavy brown wrapping paper. Have students use tempera paints to paint them. After fish are dry, staple both sides together and stuff with newspaper to make 3-D fish. Spray with fixative so that children can play with the fish without the paint rubbing off.

Day 5: Have children do a "fish act." A small group of students should hold the 3-D fish while the teacher or another student reads the poem. As each fish jumps out of the net, a student moves his/her fish to another part of the classroom.

For a related fish unit, see Teacher Created Materials #020 *Whole Language Units for Nursery Rhymes* "Fish Alive" after completing "Four Little Fishes."

Evaluate numeral matching skills by using page 55. Students will need scissors, glue, and copies of numerals 1-4 from page 8. Have them cut out numerals and paste them underneath the matching numbers. An alternate use would be for students to make sets in each box.

Provide copies of page 56 reproduced onto heavy paper. Students can glue toothpicks or twigs to make the numeral 4. Color the fish.

Little Book

My Little Book of
Four Little Fishes

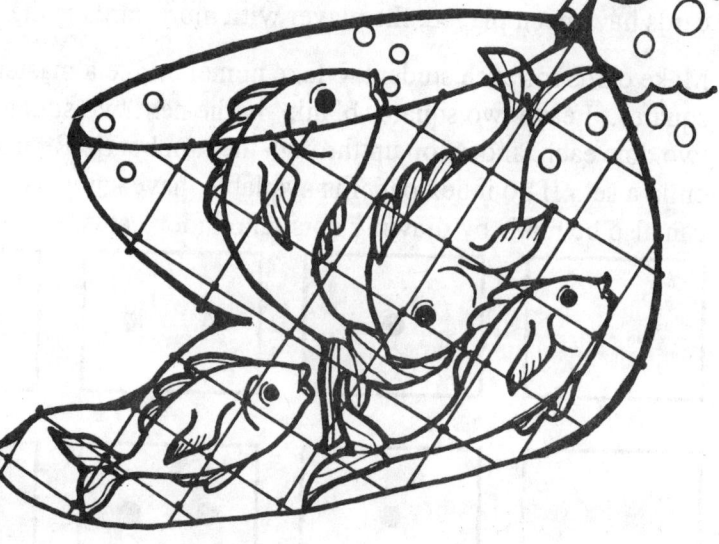

Four little fishes
Swimming in the sea.
Caught in a net,
They can't get free.

Name_____

1

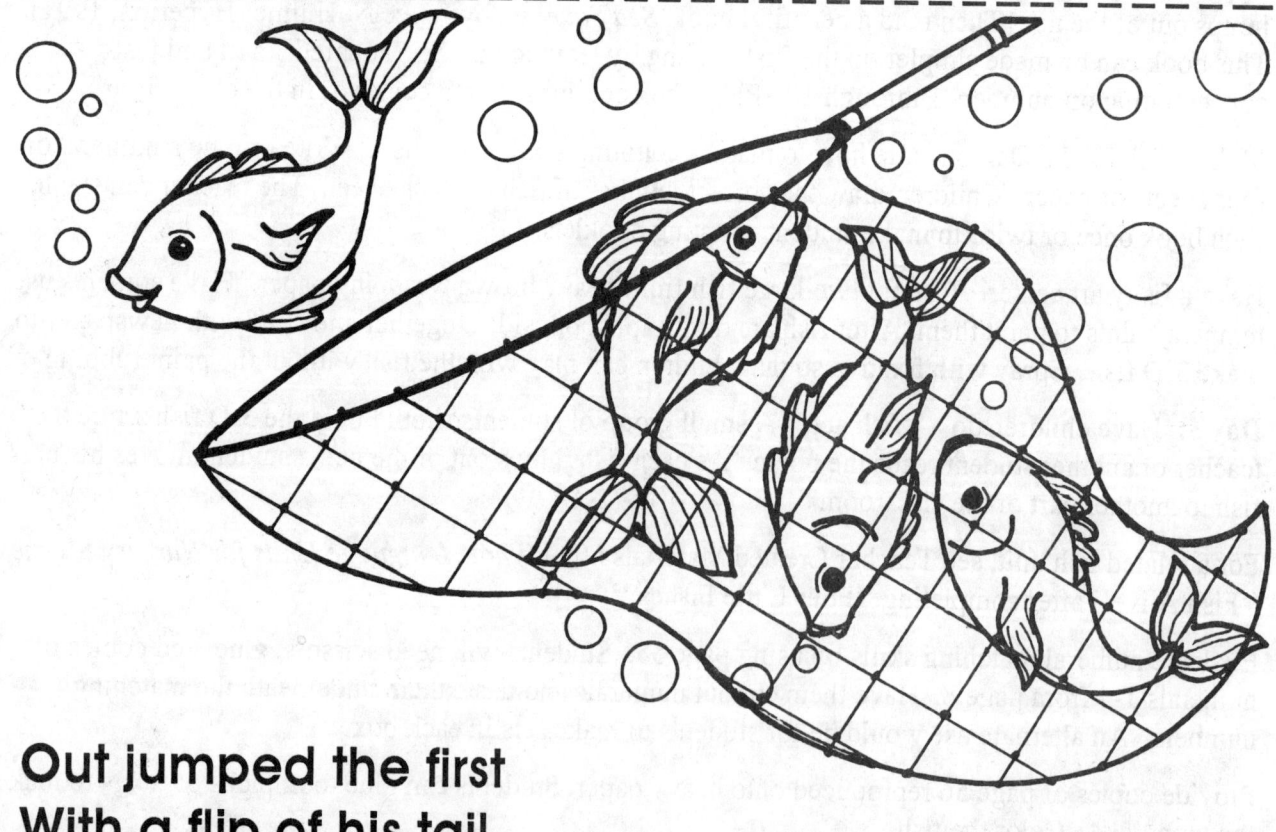

Out jumped the first
With a flip of his tail.

2

Four Little Fishes

Little Book *(cont.)*

The second one shouted,
"I can jump like a whale."

3

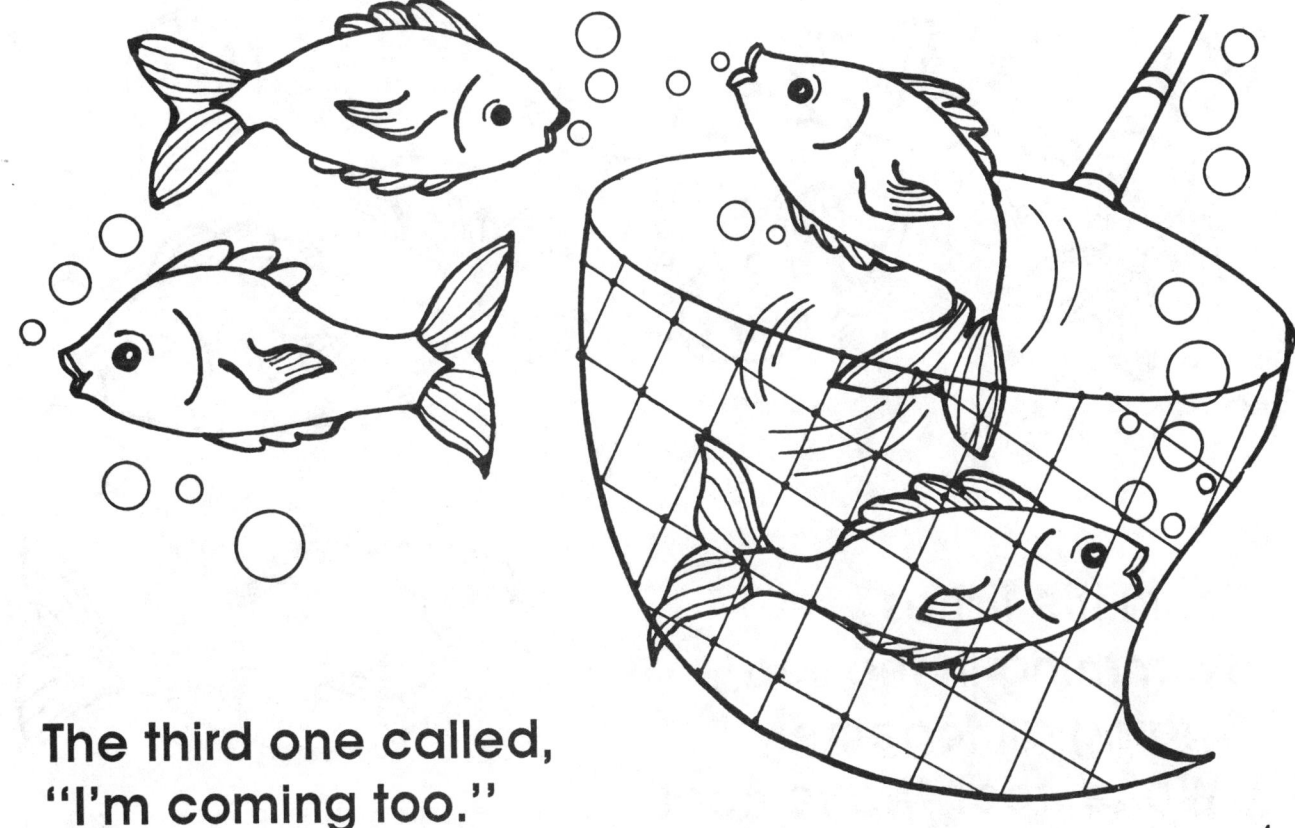

The third one called,
"I'm coming too."

4

Four Little Fishes

Little Book (cont.)

The fourth one yelled,
"I can jump like you."

5

Four little fishes
Swimming in the sea,
Singing all together,
"We're free! We're free!"

6

Four Little Fishes

Patterns

Directions: Use patterns to make five bowls and fifteen felt fish.

Four Little Fishes

Fish Drawing Lesson

1. Draw a football.
2. Add a triangle tail. 
3. Put on the eye and mouth.
4. Add a top fin.
5. Draw the fish's scales.
6. Now color your fish.

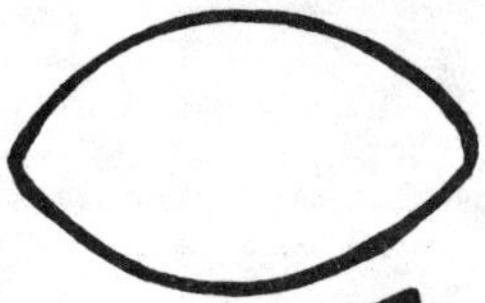

Does your fish look like this?

Four Little Fishes

Numerals Matching

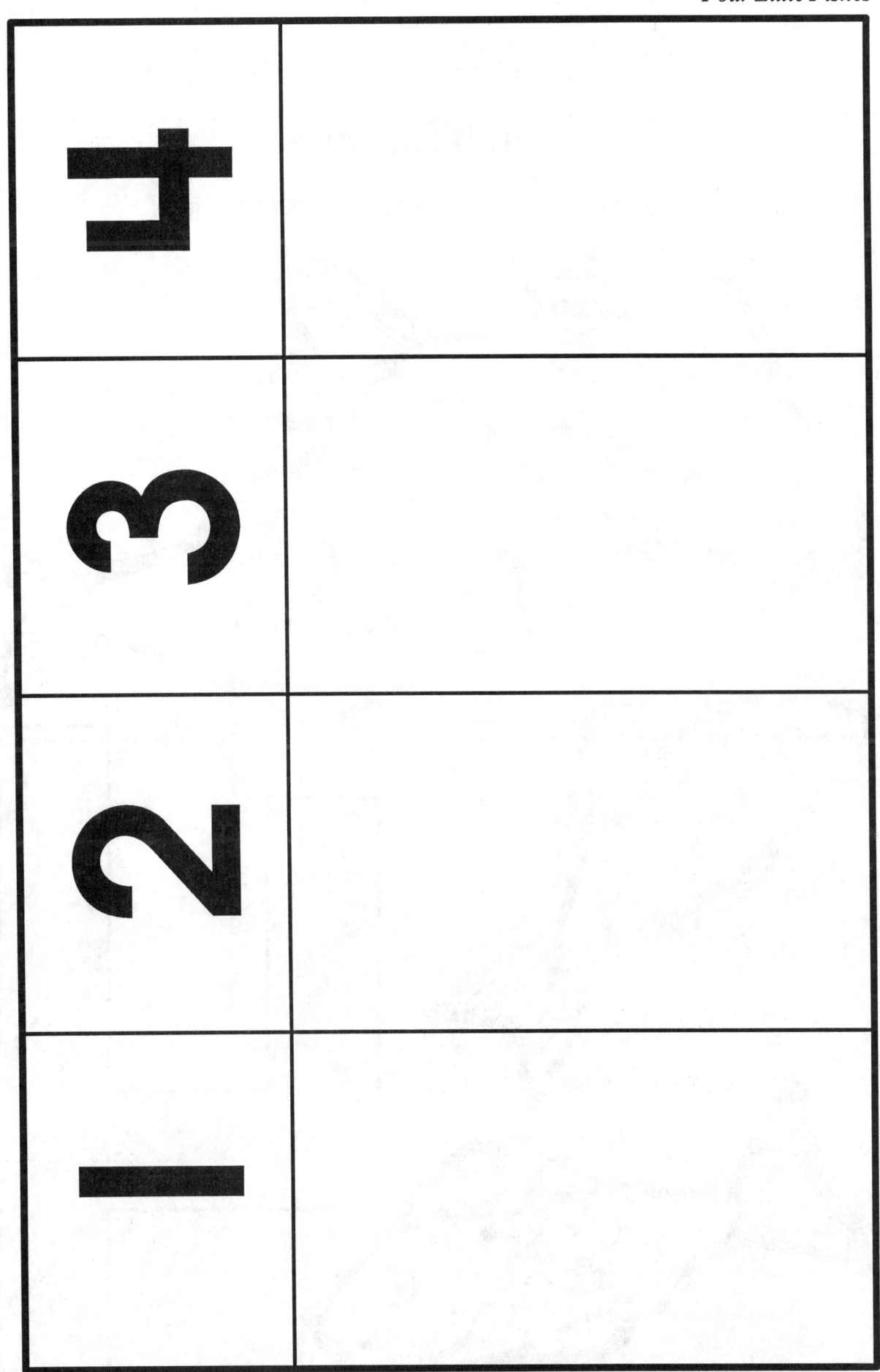

Four Little Fishes

Name:_____

Number 4

Directions: Color the fish. Glue toothpicks to the 4.

Five Little Monkeys

Five little monkeys jumping on the bed.
One fell off and bumped his head.
Mama called the doctor, and the doctor said,
"No more monkeys jumping on the bed!"

Four little monkeys jumping on the bed.
One fell off and bumped his head.
Mama called the doctor, and the doctor said,
"No more monkeys jumping on the bed!"

Three little monkeys jumping on the bed.
One fell off and bumped his head.
Mama called the doctor, and the doctor said,
"No more monkeys jumping on the bed!"

Two little monkeys jumping on the bed.
One fell off and bumped his head.
Mama called the doctor, and the doctor said,
"No more monkeys jumping on the bed!"

One little monkey jumping on the bed.
He fell off and bumped his head.
Mama called the doctor, and the doctor said,
"No more monkeys jumping on the bed!"

Five Little Monkeys

Sample Lessons

Day 1: Put up a monkey bulletin board. Use the patterns (page 65) to make five monkeys and one bed. Enlarge on the overhead or on the opaque projector. Count the monkeys on the first day; then remove a monkey on the second day. Let the students guess what happened to the monkey. Count the remaining monkeys. You may wish to add other objects to count and match.

Introduce the poem. Place the bed and five small monkeys on the flannel board. Remove one monkey as each verse is read. Follow up with a fingerplay.

Cut, color, assemble, and staple the Little Books. Encourage children to follow the text as it is read. Keep the Little Books in the children's desks so that they can read them when they finish assignments. Extra pages can be added to the end, so that children can add their own work. They can draw pictures, copy words, or write numbers. Tell them to use their imaginations.

Monkey masks can be made working with small groups in centers. Use the pattern on page 64 to let the children create monkey masks. Have them color the mask and glue it to sturdy paper. Cut out the mask after it dries and glue to tongue depressors or craft sticks. Children will need help or extra instruction to cut out the eyes. Monkey headbands can be made by gluing the monkey onto strips of paper that will fit around the children's heads.

Day 2: Reread the poem using a Big Book. Big Books can be easily made by enlarging the Little Book pages. Let the children color the pictures. Mount on poster board and laminate. Have children use their monkey masks to act out the poem. As each monkey falls off the bed, have a student sit down and hold his/her head.

Have some fun with some flannel board "monkey business." Place the five monkeys used to introduce the poem on the flannel board. Each of the monkeys has a numeral on his tummy. Make construction paper coconuts or oranges. Have students place the appropriate number of coconuts near each monkey.

Let children do some "monkey business" at the flannel board center with the monkey and bed flannel pieces. Felt or interfacing figures can be played with directly on the carpet or carpet squares if you don't have a flannel board.

Day 3: Reread the poem using the Little Books.

Share a different monkey story, *The Monkey and the Crocodile*, by Paul Galdone (Clarion, 1987).

Pretend to be jumping on the bed. Practice jumping skills outside. Using a jump rope, draw an outline of a bed (square) or draw lines in the dirt with a stick. Have children take turns jumping. Start with five children and have one jump out each time you recite the poem.

Five Little Monkeys

Sample Lessons *(cont.)*

Monkey Hat Match-Up (page 65) can be made on tag or traced onto interfacing. Reproduce hats and collars. Place 1 to 5 dots on each. Demonstrate how to play the game by placing the correct hat on each monkey by counting the dots on the collars.

Day 4: Have five different students each read one verse of the poem using a pointer with the Big Book. Others can follow along in their Little Books. Then read a related counting book, *Animal Babies, 1 2 3* by Eve Spencer (Raintree, 1990).

Introduce game board skills using a transparency of page 63. Felt numerals can be placed directly on the overhead to represent the number of spaces to be moved or make a transparency of page 63 to use as game cards. Any small object can be used as game pieces. Explain that the first animal to reach the bananas is the winner.

Make a copy of Monkey Business (page 63) for each child. Students may color the game and glue to sturdy paper to take home. Let the children practice playing the game in the classroom before taking it home. Since the winner is determined by chance, this is a good game for students to play with parents. Have students brainstorm how to play the game at home. Ask if they have any small toys or pieces from other games small enough to use as game pieces. Students should make two sets of small numeral cards to use as game cards. Use numerals 0-5 on page 8. You may wish to enlarge game boards.

Let children play in the math center. Color a copy of the game. Glue to poster board and laminate. This game can also be played with a spinner. (Blank spinners are available from teacher supply stores. Just write in the numerals 0-5.) Instruct children to select two different-colored animal counters to use as game pieces.

Day 5: Reread the poem using sentence strips in a pocket chart. Cover the numbers or use blanks for cloze exercises. If you leave a blank for the number, only one set of sentences will be needed. Each new verse can be made by simply changing the number card. Advanced students may be able to match or insert word cards.

Read *1 2 3 To the Zoo* by Eric Carle (Philomel, 1968).

Show "monkey" conservation on the flannel board. Place five monkeys far apart and six coconuts close together in a pile. Ask if there are enough coconuts for each monkey to have one. Take predictions from several students. Then have a student move the coconuts so that each monkey is holding a coconut, and the students can see that there are more than enough coconuts. In fact, there will be one coconut left over. Have students verbalize the outcome using math language. Continue using oranges, apples, etc.

Little Book

My Little Book of
Five Little Monkeys

Name: _____

Five little monkeys jumping on the bed.
One fell off and bumped his head.

1

Mama called the doctor, and the doctor said,
"No more monkeys jumping on the bed!"

2

Little Book (cont.)

Four little monkeys jumping on the bed.
One fell off and bumped his head.
Mama called the doctor, and the doctor said,
"No more monkeys jumping on the bed!"

3

Three little monkeys jumping on the bed.
One fell off and bumped his head.
Mama called the doctor, and the doctor said,
"No more monkeys jumping on the bed!"

4

Little Book (cont.)

Two little monkeys jumping on the bed.
One fell off and bumped his head.
Mama called the doctor, and the doctor said,
"No more monkeys jumping on the bed!"

5

One little monkey jumping on the bed.
He fell off and bumped his head.
Mama called the doctor, and the doctor said,
"No more monkeys jumping on the bed!"

6

Five Little Monkeys

Directions: Two people may play. Use two coins, buttons, or small lids for game pieces. Place game pieces on start. Place number cards on board. Players take turns drawing top card, moving until one reaches finish. The first one to reach the bananas wins.

Five Little Monkeys

Monkey Mask

Use this pattern as a mask by taping it to a craft stick or tongue depressor or use as a headband.

Five Little Monkeys

Patterns

©1993 Teacher Created Materials, Inc. 65 #200 Whole Language Units for Math

Five Little Monkeys

Name _____

Monkey Match

Will all the monkeys get a banana? Will there be any bananas left over? Draw lines to match each monkey to a banana.

#200 Whole Language Units for Math ©1993 Teacher Created Materials, Inc.

Five Little Monkeys

Name:_____

Number 5

Directions: Color the monkeys. Glue rice to the 5.

©1993 Teacher Created Materials, Inc. #200 Whole Language Units for Math

I Bought the Circus

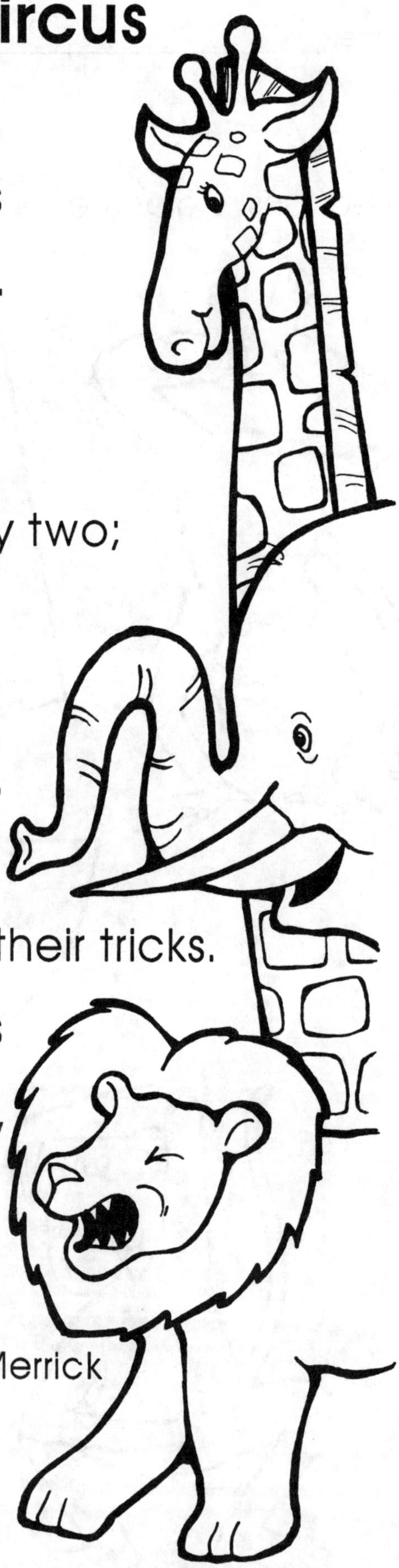

I dreamed I bought the circus

When I went to bed last night.

I didn't need a ticket

To see the thrilling sight.

The elephants came in two by two;

It's much better than the zoo.

The lions came in four by four;

Listen to them growl and roar.

The seals came in six by six,

Bounced some balls and did their tricks.

I dreamed I bought the circus

When I went to bed last night,

And now instead of sleeping,

I watch it every night.

by Sandra Merrick

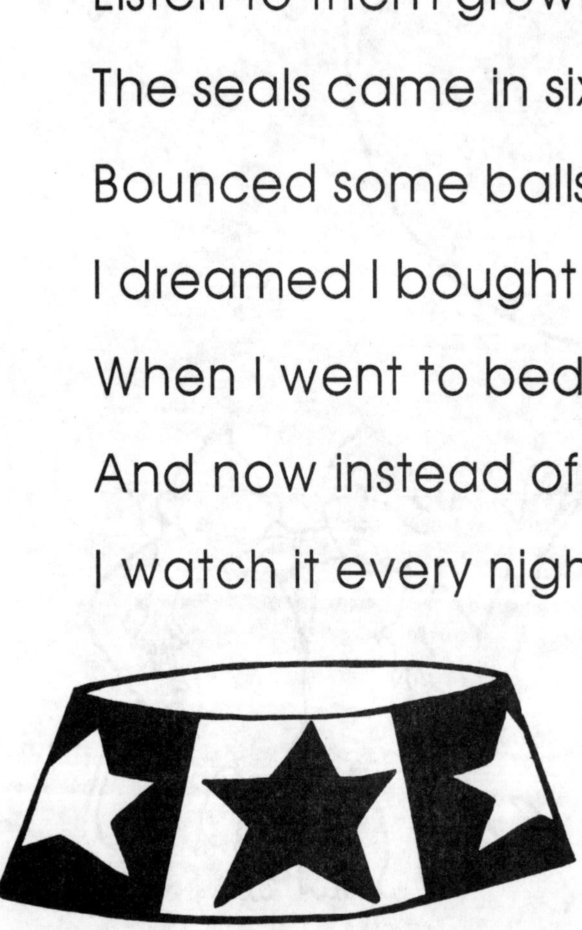

I Bought the Circus

Sample Lessons

Day 1: Prepare a circus bulletin board. Enlarge two elephants on gray or light blue tag. Continue with four lions and six seals. Place the numeral cards 2, 4, and 6 near each set of animals. Use the title "Counting Circus." Students can make animals to add to the board (for example: 5 snakes, 1 monkey, 3 dogs). The numbers can be changed to provide counting activities.

Introduce the poem using transparencies on the overhead projector. Discuss the meaning of the poem and explain that the child had the same dream every night. Place the numeral cards 2, 4, and 6 on the chalkboard ledge and ask what numerals are missing in the counting order. Let students place numeral cards in the correct places. At story time, follow up by reading circus and animal books. A good selection is *Curious George Rides a Bike* by H.A. Rey (Houghton Mifflin, 1973).

Day 2: Do "seal tricks" on the flannel board. Place a seal on the flannel board with six felt circles. Explain that seals can do all kinds of juggling and balancing tricks with their noses. Have a student count the balls and select the numeral 6. Arrange the balls in different formations to show the many different ways to make six. Make up little stories:

> The seal was balancing 3 balls on his nose, and then the trainer threw him 3 more balls. How many balls does he have now? The seal was juggling 4 balls, and 2 balls were on the ground. How many balls are on the board?

Can seals count? Have students complete the worksheet on page 74. Color the seal and draw 6 balls for the seal to juggle.

Complete the worksheet. Color the seals and glue yarn to the numeral 6 on page 75. The yarn will have to be measured and precut by the teacher.

Day 3: Reread the poem each day using an overhead or a teacher prepared Big Book.

Have the students count by 2's. A fun way to do this is to line the children up two by two and then have them count off.

Let students discuss circuses they have seen in person, on television, or read about in books.

Day 4: Do some cloze activities. Read the poem first and leave out some numbers. Next try leaving out some rhyming words.

Complete Little Books by letting children assemble the Little Books on pages 70-72.

Prepare and demonstrate materials for centers. Seals sit on blocks or platforms so that they can be seen by the audience. Place a different numeral on six platforms and have the students place the corresponding number of balls on the seal's nose. Use seals and platforms on worksheet page 75 as patterns. Use small circles to make six balls. See Using the Patterns on page 5 for ideas.

Let children play circus. Place toy zoo animals in blocks and stuffed animals in the house.

Little Book

My Little Book of
I Bought the Circus

Name _____

I dreamed I bought the circus
When I went to bed last night.
I didn't need a ticket
To see the thrilling sight.

1

I Bought the Circus

Little Book (cont.)

The elephants came in two by two;
It's much better than the zoo.

2

The lions came in four by four;
Listen to them growl and roar.

3

Little Book (cont.)

The seals came in six by six,
Bounced some balls and did their tricks.

I dreamed I bought the circus
When I went to bed last night,
And now instead of sleeping,
I watch it every night.

I Bought the Circus

Patterns

I Bought the Circus

Name: _____

Circus Seals and Balls

Directions: Draw 6 balls for the seals. Color the seals and balls

I Bought the Circus

Name:_____

Number 6

Directions: Glue a piece of yarn to the 6. Color the seals.

©1993 Teacher Created Materials, Inc. 75 #200 Whole Language Units for Math

Going to St. Ives

As I was going to St. Ives

I met a man with seven wives.

Every wife had seven sacks,

Every sack had seven cats,

Every cat had seven kits.

Kits, cats, sacks, and wives,

How many were going to St. Ives?

Going to St. Ives

Sample Lessons

Day 1: Prepare a cat bulletin board by enlarging the cat pattern on page 81. Make seven cats on orange, yellow, and white tag. You may wish to attach cats to the bulletin board and let students draw on spots or stripes. Outline spots and stripes with a marker. Supply numeral cards 1-7. Have students place cards in order under cats, using push pins. Use letters or a banner to title the board: Going to St. Ives.

Introduce the nursery rhyme using a Big Book or transparencies. Explain that the poem is a riddle. Reread and ask how many were going to St. Ives. Ask how many people are indicated by the word, "I." (Answer: 1) Follow up by reading *Millions of Cats* by Wanda Gag (Putnam, 1977) or sharing other Mother Goose rhymes about cats such as "The Kilkenny Cats" and "The Gingham Dog and the Calico Cat." Two good stories about seven are "Snow White and the Seven Dwarves" and "The Wolf and Seven Little Kids."

Day 2: Count cats. Place a wife on the flannel board and display the numeral 7. Use a picture of a wife from the worksheet on page 83 as a pattern. Students place seven sacks on the flannel board. (Use felt triangles or circles.) Have another student place seven felt cats on the board. Then have a third student place seven felt kittens on the board. (To see if students understand the concept of seven, have 8 to 10 of each item to see if the students continue or stop at 7.)

Use a pegboard to demonstrate a number stair. Build a number stair on the flannel board using felt squares.

Day 3: Give each child ten beans or buttons. Hold up large numeral cards while students form appropriate sets with buttons. On the next day, give each child a handful of buttons. Place buttons on page 82 to form a number stair. On the next day, students color squares to make a number stair.

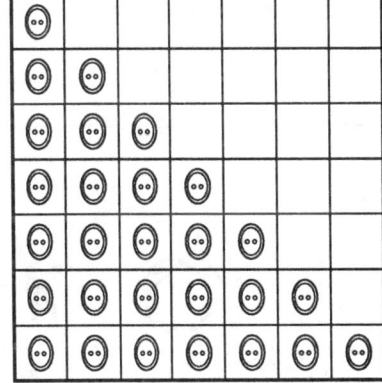

Use the other worksheets in the unit. Draw seven sacks for the wife on page 83. Color cats. Cut and glue straws on the seven on page 84.

Day 4: Reread the nursery rhyme each day. Count the cats on the bulletin board. What is a kit? How many kittens does one cat have?

How many days in a week? Look at the calendar. Talk about cats and why they make good pets. Do cloze leaving out "cat," "cats," and "seven."

Complete Little Books.

Prepare and demonstrate materials for centers. Encourage students to make number stairs on pegboards, felt squares on flannel board, and with counting cubes.

Little Book

My Little Book of
Going to St. Ives

Name: _____

As I was going to St. Ives
I met a man with seven wives.

1

Going to St. Ives

Little Book (cont.)

Every wife had seven sacks,

2

Every sack had seven cats,

3

Going to St.Ives

Little Book (cont.)

Every cat had seven kits.

4

Kits, cats, sacks, and wives,
How many were going to St. Ives?

5

Going to St. Ives

Patterns

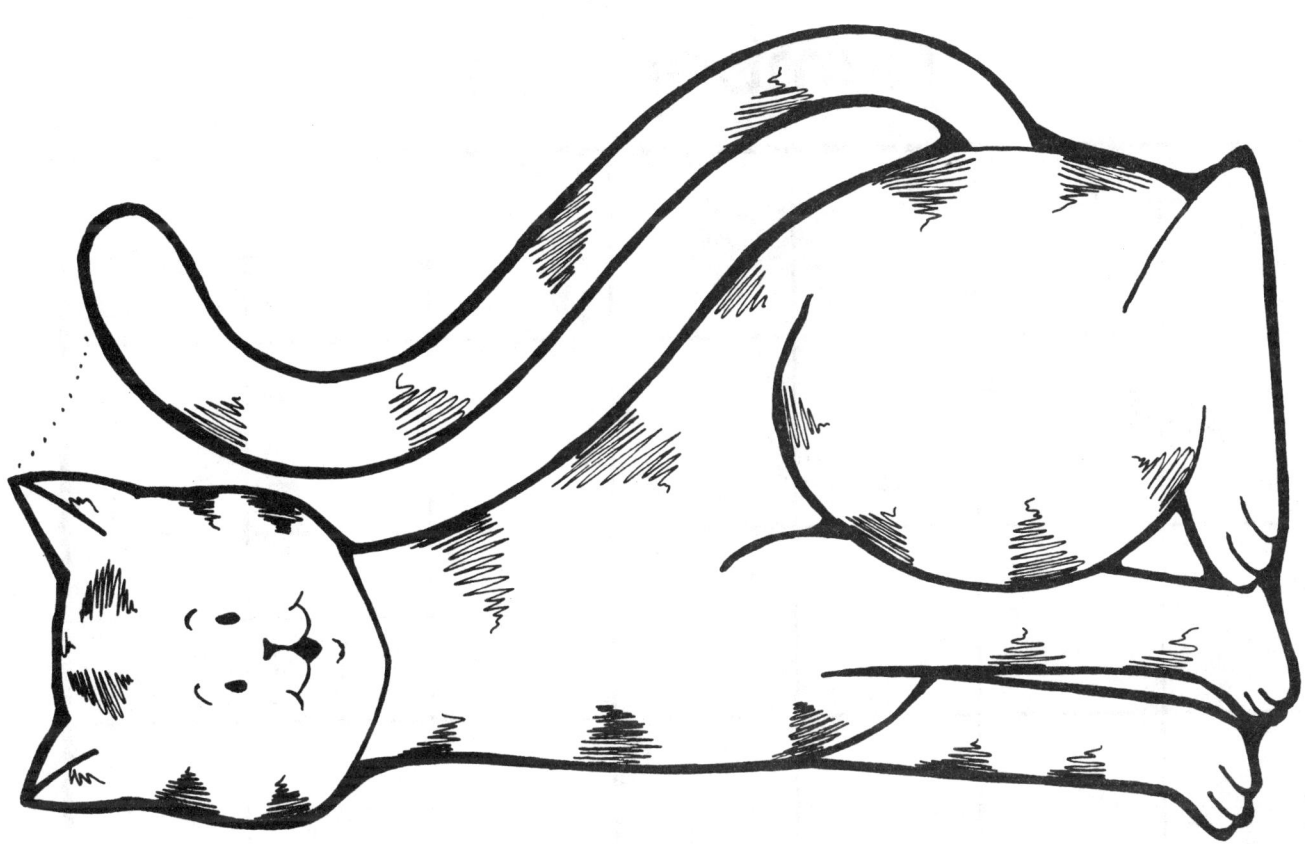

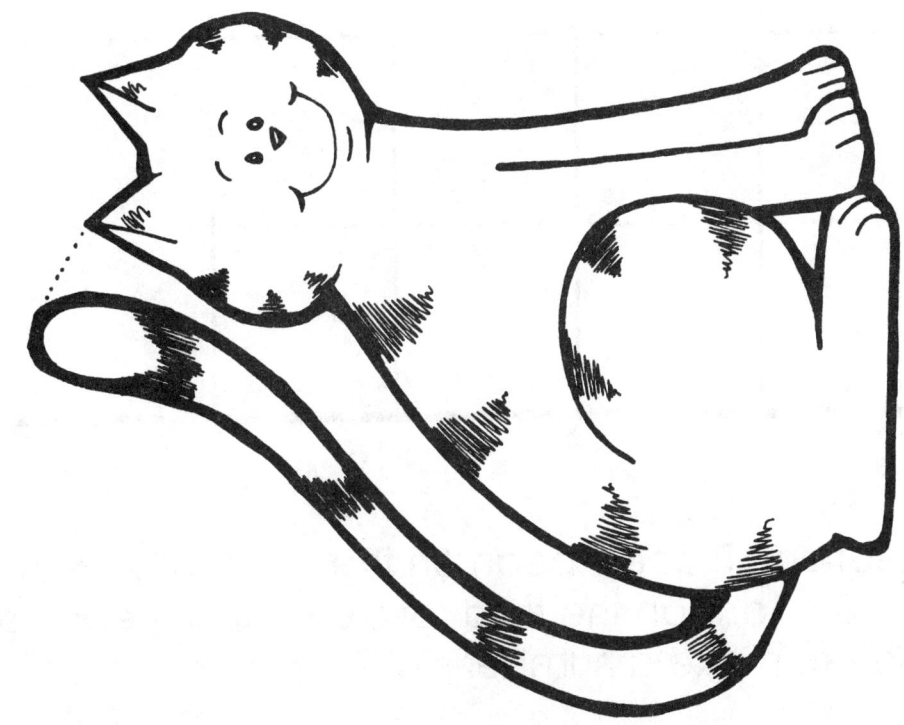

Going to St. Ives

Name _____

Number Stair

Directions: Place 1 bean on the top row, 2 beans on the second row, 3 beans on the third row, etc. Color each square with a bean to make a number stair.

Going to St. Ives

Name:_____

Sacks and Wives

Directions: Draw 7 sacks for this wife. You may draw rectangles for sacks. Color.

Going to St. Ives

Name:_____

Number 7

Directions: Color the cats. Cut paper or plastic straws to glue onto the number 7.

An Old Man with a Beard

There was an old man with a beard,

Who said, ``It is just as I feared! —

Two owls and a hen,

Four larks and a wren,

Have all built their nests in my beard.''

— Edward Lear

An Old Man with a Beard

Sample Lessons

Day 1: Enlarge the old man's face on page 91 to create a bulletin-board-sized "beard." Cut a long wavy piece of white bulletin board paper for the beard. Place birds from page 90 in the beard with push pins. Have a student count the birds and choose the correct numeral card. If you wish, you can change the number of birds each day and have a child select the correct numeral. Title the bulletin board "Birds in a Beard."

Introduce the limerick using a Big Book or transparencies. After reading the limerick, reread "The Kilkenny Cats," which is similar in style to a limerick. On following days read another story featuring a beard, "Snow White and Rose Red." Mother Goose has several poems about eight; one of these is "Wee Willie Winkie." Here is another Mother Goose rhyme about eight:

> *Cantaloupes! Cantaloupes! What is the price?*
>
> *Eight for a dollar, and all very nice.*

Make sure the children know what a cantaloupe is. If you serve small pieces, one cantaloupe will provide a taste for the whole class.

Work with the concept of more or less. Make trees, larks, owls, hen, and wren from felt using the patterns on page 90. Place one hen and two owls on the flannel board. Which set is more? Which set is less? Explain that 2 is 1 more than 1. Do the same for two owls and three larks. Explain that 3 is 1 more than 2. Use all the birds in the limerick (8). Match birds to trees sets using the words "more" and "less." Match birds to eggs.

Day 2: Reread the poem using the Big Book.

Model page 92 with felt figures on the flannel board. Explain that there must be equal (or same) numbers of birds and eggs. Then have children complete the page.

Day 3: Practice drawing sets with one more on the chalkboard. For example, draw three circles on the board, then have a student draw a set with four circles. Repeat with two triangles; then four ovals. Then have children complete page 93.

Complete the numeral worksheet on page 94. Glue macaroni to the 8 and color the birds.

Day 4: Reread the limerick each day. Ask what kinds of birds make good pets? Look at a bird book.

How many crayons are in the small crayon box? Pass one or two boxes around. Notice that some children will count the crayons, and some will read the numeral on the box.

Do cloze by covering the words "man" and "beard." Cover more words on subsequent days.

Complete Little Books.

Prepare and demonstrate materials for centers.

Have partners play the "more game." Use counters or cubes from your math center. One student makes a set, then the other child makes a set with one more.

Encourage students to make up stories using the birds and other flannel board figures.

Little Book

My Little Book of
An Old Man with a Beard

Name:_____

There was an old man with a beard,

1

An Old Man with a Beard

Little Book (cont.)

Who said,
"It is just as I feared! —

2

Two owls and a hen,

3

An Old Man with a Beard

Little Book (cont.)

Four larks and a wren,

4

Have all built their nests in my beard."

5

An Old Man with a Beard

Patterns

An Old Man with a Beard

Patterns *(cont.)*

An Old Man with a Beard

Name:_____

Eggs and Birds

Match birds to eggs by drawing lines. How many birds are there? _____ How many eggs are there? _____

An Old Man with a Beard

Name:_____

One More

Directions: Draw a set with one more.

 men	
 trees	
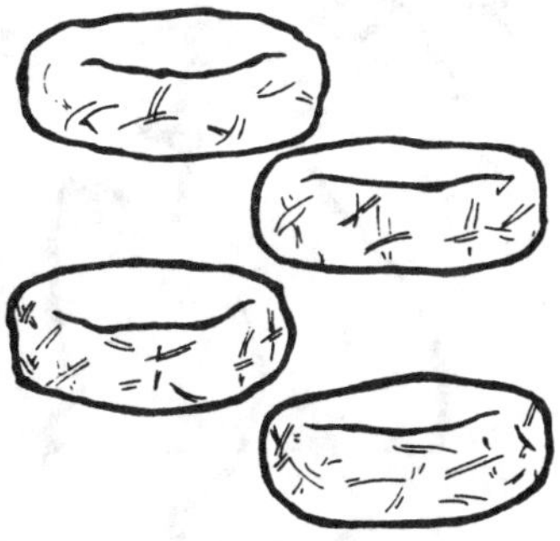 nests	

©1993 Teacher Created Materials, Inc. 93 #200 Whole Language Units for Math

An Old Man with a Beard

Name:_____

Number 8

Directions: Color the birds. Glue macaroni to the 8.

Nine Ponies

Pretty ponies, look so fine;

Nine ponies in a line,

Bathed and brushed until they shine.

Mother told me not to whine,

But how I wish they could be mine.

                    by Sandra Merrick

Nine Ponies

Sample Lessons

Day 1: Prepare a pony bulletin board by enlarging pony pattern on page 100 using different colors of tag to save time on coloring. Make 9 barns on red tag by copying the pattern on page 100. On each barn door write a numeral 1 through 9. Under each pony attach a small container. Have students place the barns in counting order under the ponies.

Introduce the poem using a Big Book or transparencies. Discuss pony rides and where children might see them. Contrast the live ponies with the ponies on a carousel.

Day 2: Make felt or interfacing ponies for the flannel board. Use a fine point permanent marker to write the numerals 1 through 9 on their saddles. Scramble the ponies and let students place them in counting order. It may be necessary to place them in two rows. Place in a center.

Teach children to play tic-tac-toe emphasizing that tic-tac-toe is played in a nine-square grid.

Day 3: Tell the children that they are going to design their own math projects. Place squares on the flannel board with numerals to match. Explain that this is one idea they might use, but that they are free to do anything they wish as long as they can explain it. Some children might not know what math is. Give examples of some of the things they have learned in math: counting, numerals, sorting, patterns, number stairs, etc. Give each child a copy of page 8, a 12" x 18" (30 cm x 46 cm) sheet of manila paper, scissors, and glue. Cut shapes from colored paper.

Make copies of page 101 for each child. Glue the 9 at the top of a piece of construction paper. Then glue ten pony ride tickets on the paper. Remind the students to count carefully. Don't tell them that there are more than nine tickets on the page. Let them discover it. To insure success, practice this lesson on the flannel board first using 10 or 12 felt rectangles to represent ride tickets. Give each child more than nine tickets when it is his/her turn. Repeat with other numbers if you wish.

Day 4: Glue glitter on the 9 on page 102.

Match the barns to the ponies on the bulletin board.

Read *Blaze and the Gray Spotted Pony* (Macmillan, 1968), *Blaze and the Forest Fire* (1969), or any other book featuring the pony Blaze, all written by Clarence Anderson.

Have children tell you numbers less than and more than nine.

Complete Little Books. Reread the poem finding the words pony, ponies, nine.

Prepare and demonstrate materials for centers. Place numeral cards 1 through 9 in the center. Have a large number of felt rectangles to use for pony ride tickets. Match the correct number of tickets to the numeral.

Little Book

My Little Book of
Nine Ponies

Name: _____

Pretty ponies,
look so fine;

Nine Ponies

Little Book (cont.)

Nine ponies in a line,

2

Bathed and brushed until they shine.

3

Little Book (cont.)

Mother told me not to whine,

4

But how I wish they could be mine.

5

Nine Ponies

Patterns

Nine Ponies

Name _____

Take a Pony Ride

Directions: Cut out the 9 and glue it to another sheet. Count and cut out 9 pony ride tickets. Glue them to the other sheet.

©1993 Teacher Created Materials, Inc. #200 Whole Language Units for Math

Nine Ponies

Name:_____

Number 9

Directions: Color the ponies. Glue glitter or grits to the 9.

Penguin Parade

Penguins marching one by one;
Come along and have some fun.
Penguins marching two by two;
It's so cold, they're turning blue.
Penguins marching three by three,
Until they dive into the sea.
Penguins marching four by four;
They come sliding through the door.
Penguins marching five by five;
Some will walk, and some will drive.
Penguins marching six by six;
Watch them do some silly tricks.
Penguins marching seven by seven;
Cold, cold snow feels like heaven.
Penguins marching eight by eight;
Hurry! Hurry! Don't be late!
Penguins marching nine by nine;
Everybody, stay in line.
Penguins marching ten by ten;
Dive and slide and swim again.

by Sandra Merrick

Penguin Parade

Sample Lessons

Day 1: Prepare the bulletin board. Make ten copies or enlargements of the penguin pattern on page 111. Write or glue numerals 1–10 on penguin tummies. Cut white bulletin board paper for hills of snow. Students can add snowflakes.

Introduce the poem using a Big Book or transparencies of the Little Book pages. Ask if anyone knows some songs or stories about 10. Follow up by singing the Mother Goose rhyme "This Old Man."

Day 2: Make penguin puppets by copying the pattern on page 111 on poster board. On each write a numeral 1 through 10. Laminate and tape to tongue depressors or craft sticks. Have ten students act out the poem. Point to each child as his/her number is read and have each stand up. As students return puppets, have each read the number on his/her puppet. Repeat with ten more students.

Read *Ten, Nine, Eight* by Molly Bang (Greenwillow, 1991). Place numeral cards 1–10 in a pocket chart or on the chalkboard ledge. Practice counting backwards while pointing to the numeral cards. Then have students count backwards for the class.

Play the penguin matching game on page 110. Match the penguins to the correct snowmobile.

Day 3: Have students create another math project. Suggest they create sets and then write the numeral. Some may wish to illustrate counting backwards. Ask them not to repeat the project they did for the Nine Ponies unit. Provide a large piece of paper for the project. Use page 113 as an evaluation for matching numerals to sets

Day 4: Reread the poem.

Play "Count up, Countdown" from Hap Palmer's *Math Readiness* album. Learn other types of counting, such as counting by 2's and 10's. Count to 100. Look at a 1 to 100 chart.

Complete Little Books.

This poem is excellent for cloze activities. Begin by leaving out the rhyming words. As children become more confident, leave out more words. Copy some sentences on index cards and pass out to students so they can place them in order in a pocket chart.

Little Book

My Little Book of
Penguin Parade

Name: _____

**Penguins marching one by one;
Come along and have some fun.**

1

**Penguins marching two by two;
It's so cold, they're turning blue.**

2

Little Book (cont.)

Penguins marching three by three,
Until they dive into the sea.

3

Penguins marching four by four;
They come sliding through the door.

4

Little Book (cont.)

Penguins marching five by five;
Some will walk, and some will drive.

5

Penguins marching six by six;
Watch them do some silly tricks.

6

Penguin Parade

Little Book (cont.)

**Penguins marching seven by seven;
Cold, cold snow feels like heaven.**

7

**Penguins marching eight by eight;
Hurry! Hurry! Don't be late!**

8

Little Book (cont.)

Penguins marching nine by nine;
Everybody, stay in line.

Penguins marching ten by ten;
Dive and slide and swim again.

Penguin Parade

Name _____

Penguin Parade

Directions: Can each penguin ride in a snowmobile? Draw a line from each penguin to the snowmobiles to find out.

#200 Whole Language Units for Math ©1993 Teacher Created Materials, Inc.

Penguin Parade

Penguin Puppet Pattern

Make ten penguins on poster board. Write or glue a numeral 1–10 on each penguin. Laminate and tape to craft sticks or tongue depressors.

Penguin Parade

Name:_____

Number 10

Directions: Color penguins. Glue salt or sugar to the number 10.

Penguin Parade

How Many Are There?

Directions: Write the correct numeral in each box.

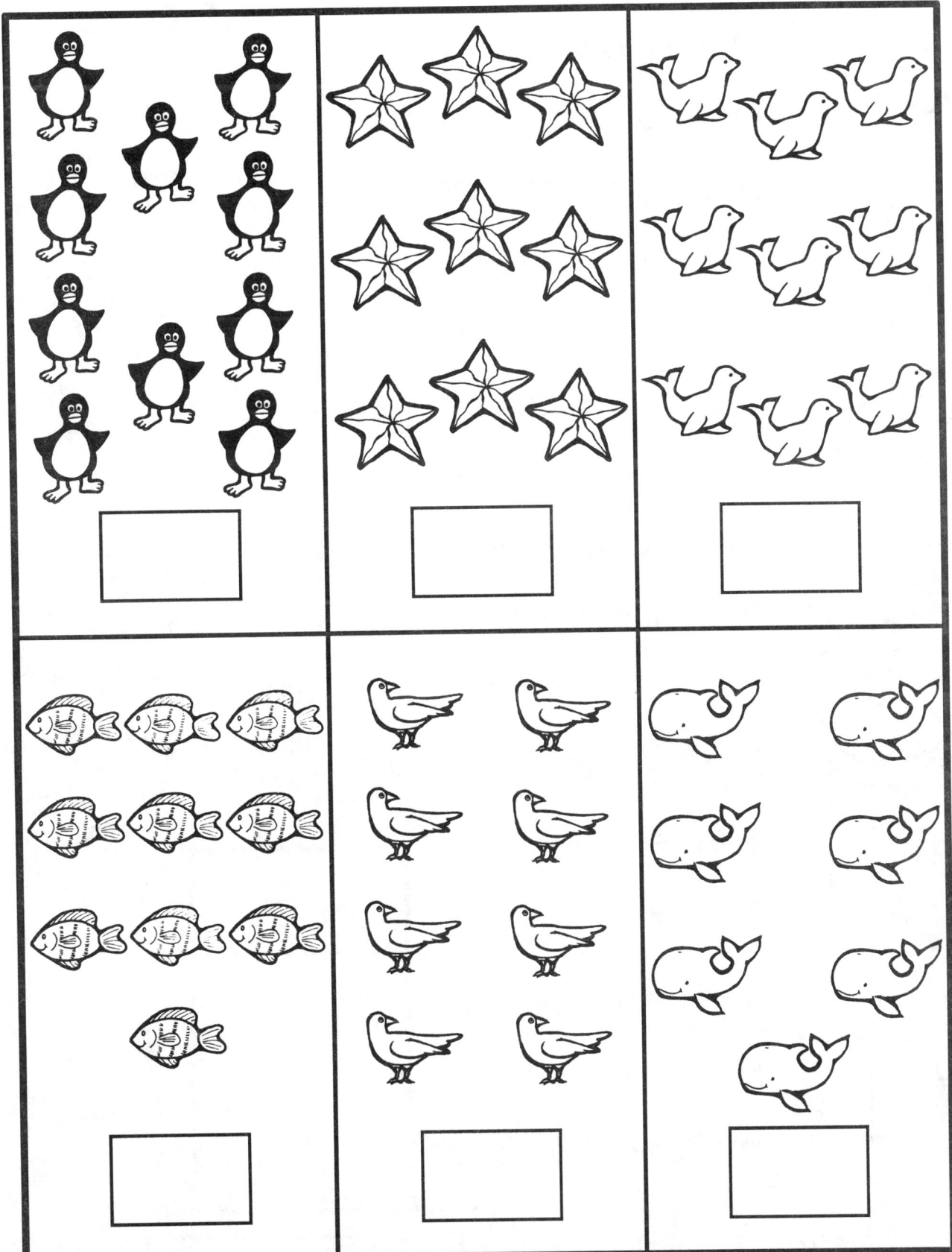

Doubles

One plus one is two;

One for me, and one for you.

Two plus two is four;

Like four corners on a door.

Three plus three is six;

Learn to add with counting sticks.

Four plus four is eight;

I think you're doing great.

Five plus five is ten;

Let's go back and start again.

1 + 1 = 2

2 + 2 = 4

3 + 3 = 6

4 + 4 = 8

5 + 5 = 10

by Sandra Merrick

Doubles

Sample Lessons

Day 1: Make flannel board pieces from the patterns on pages 122-123 and addition cards out of interfacing on page 126.

Make a Big Book for "Doubles." Print text on left page. On the right page, print the problem. Use pictures from pattern pages for illustrations. The illustrations should appear on the right-hand page under the problems. An alternate method for making the Big Book is to enlarge the Little Book pages on a copier and glue to heavy stock. Have students or parent volunteers color, then laminate. The Big Book should differ from the Little Books in that the problems on the last page of the Big Book should include the answers.

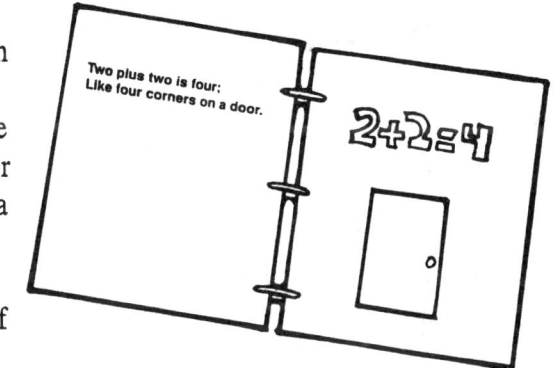

Introduce "Doubles" using the Big Book. Explain that "+" means to put together or join. Demonstrate addition using felt manipulatives on the flannel board. Display the teacher set of addition cards made from interfacing and tell the children that the cards are how we write down what we did.

Use the patterns on page 126 to make interfacing addition cards from Pellon 930. Place Pellon over patterns and trace with a fine point permanent marker. Cut with scissors and use on flannel board. Make two sets so that the students will have a set to use in centers and the teacher will have a set for demonstration. On the student set, cut the interfacing card so that the problem and the answer appear on two different pieces. During centers the children can work on the flannel board to match the answer to the problem.

Reread the poem while displaying the interfacing addition cards. Pause at the end of each phrase and let a student select the correct interfacing card.

Make a "Doubles" folder game for students to use in centers. (See patterns on pages 122-123.) Students already know how to make an apple folder; modify the apple folder to use with Doubles. Students can make a folder game to take home.

In the math center one child uses the folder, while another checks it. Another pair of students can work with the Big Book and the flannel board. One student can read the Big Book aloud while another models the text with felt manipulatives and interfacing addition cards on flannel board. It will probably be necessary for the teacher to model these behaviors since young children are inexperienced in working together. Explain to the children that they can take turns in each role.

Day 2: Reread "Doubles." After reading the book, tape a long piece of paper over the answers on the back page. Challenge the group to read the equations and provide the correct answers.

Take the class on a walk to collect small natural objects for counting, adding, and subtracting. Have each child carry a small paper bag to collect rocks, pebbles, twigs, leaves, and seeds. (If this is not possible, use the patterns at the bottom of page 117.) Return to class and use the objects as manipulatives for math problems, letting children make up problems for others to solve.

Doubles

Sample Lessons *(cont.)*

At the math center, continue activities from Day 1. Allow the children to take the manipulatives from their nature walk to the math center with them. Ask them if they can use the natural objects to show the problems in "Doubles." Encourage them to make up stories like the ones done on the flannel board.

Let children use washable markers to color the playground picture on page 124 to use as you give them problems using the manipulatives they have collected. For example:

- You found 4 twigs beside the bush and 4 twigs under the tree. How many twigs did you find?
- You found 5 pebbles in front of the swings and 5 pebbles on the sidewalk. How many pebbles did you find?
- You found 1 big rock by the slide and 1 more big rock by the fence. How many rocks did you find?
- You found 3 seeds in the grass and 3 seeds beside the bush. How many seeds did you find?
- You found 2 leaves near the big tree and 2 beside the swings. How many leaves did you find?

Listen to Hap Palmer's excellent album, *Addition and Subtraction*. "Do You Know?" is a song about addition which teaches the commutative property.

Day 3: Recite "Doubles" as you place felt manipulatives or real objects on the overhead. Many objects from the math center work well on the overhead: interlocking cubes, counting sticks, counters, nature objects. Inch graph paper can be made into transparencies to represent all types of cubes on the overhead.

Let each child make a Little Book. Reproduce pages 118-121 for each child. Students color the Little Books, and use the page numbers to place pages in order. Check page order and staple each book. Read the books repeatedly in class. Enlarge, color, and laminate one copy of the Little Book for the math center if you wish. The last page is blank for student activities. Students may copy numbers, equations, draw sets, or create their own math project. Challenge some students to create and write new equations such as $2 + 1 = 3$. Use the Little Books in class for about a week and then send them home to share.

Demonstrate how to use linking cubes and other commercial manipulatives to show doubles. Hold two red cubes on one finger and two blue cubes on another. Connect all four cubes while reminding the children that "+" means to join. Repeat using all the equations in "Doubles." Display the whole set. Ask students if they can use cubes or other materials to show doubles in the math center. Challenge them to match their joined sets to the appropriate interfacing addition card by laying each set next to the correct addition card.

Doubles

Sample Lessons *(cont.)*

Day 4: Reread the Big Book. Do some cloze activities. Tape a piece of note paper over the answer on each page. As you read each couplet, pause at the end of the first line. Example: One plus one is _____. Later in the unit, you might try covering the addends as a special challenge.

Use A Class Act. See page 125 for complete directions.

Give each child a piece of 1" graph paper. Pass out glue and 11" x 17" (28 cm x 43 cm) stiff paper and glue. Tell students to create their own math projects on the large paper using the paper strips. Suggest that they might want to show doubles. After each child finishes, let each explain his/her project. The explanation is essential to evaluation. Accept any project that can be reasonably explained. See example:

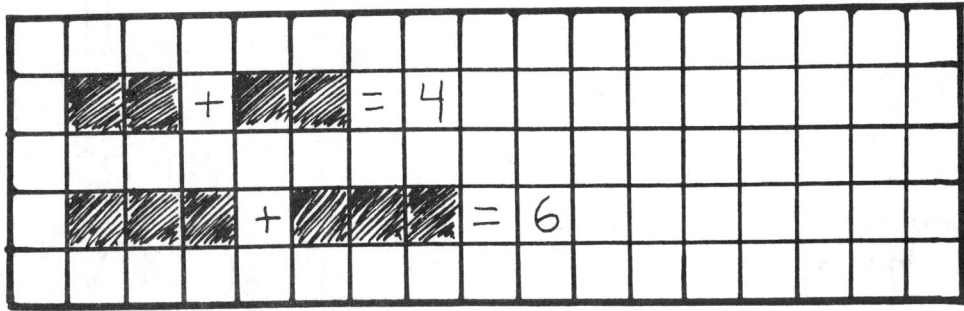

Day 5: Let a student read the "Doubles" Big Book to the class as the teacher indicates the text with a pointer.

Use Doubles Match, page 127, as an evaluation for the whole class.

Nature Patterns

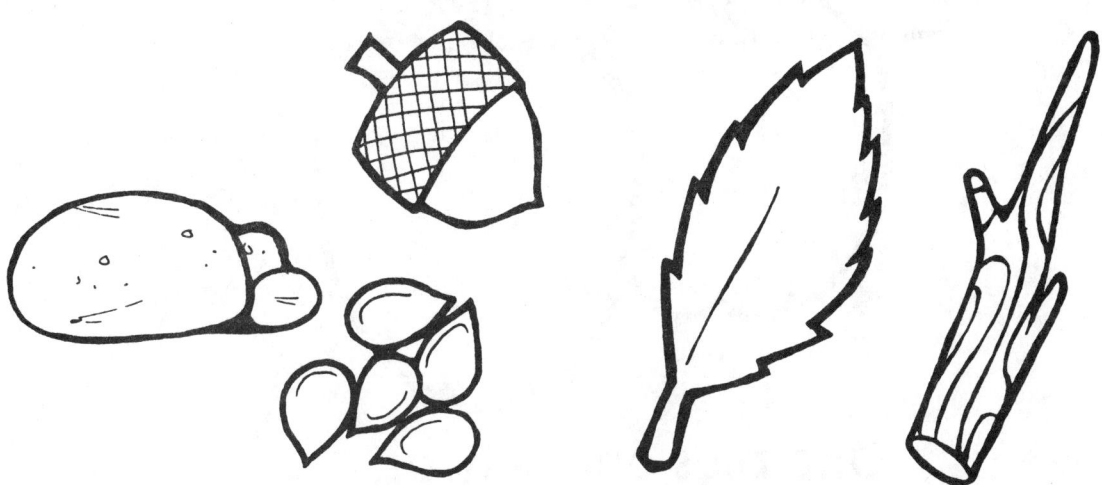

Doubles

Little Book

My Little Book of
Doubles

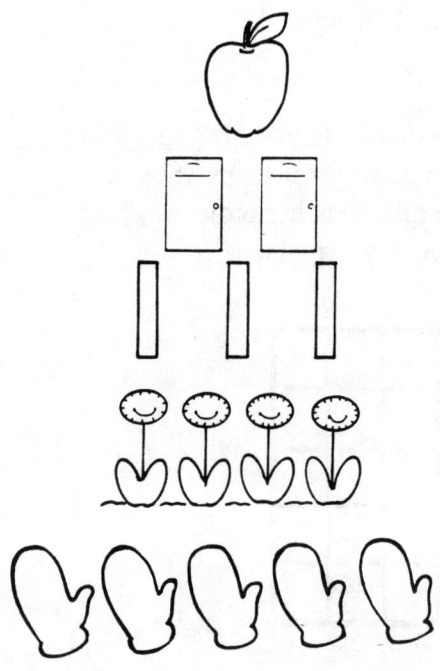
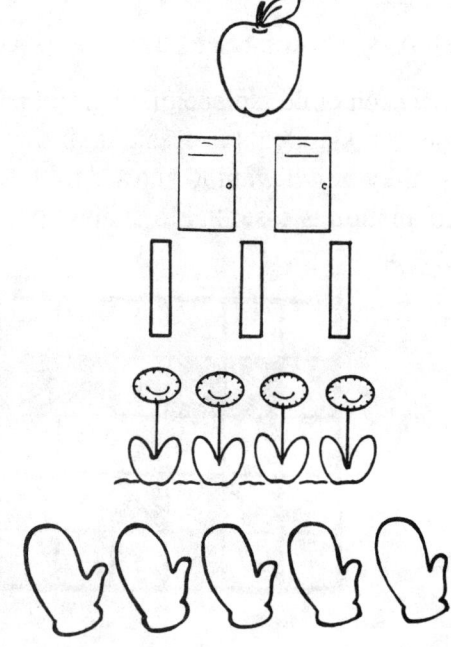

Name _____

1 + 1 = 2

One plus one is two;
One for me, and one for you.

1

Doubles

Little Book (cont.)

2 + 2 = 4

Two plus two is four;
Like four corners on a door.

2

3 + 3 = 6

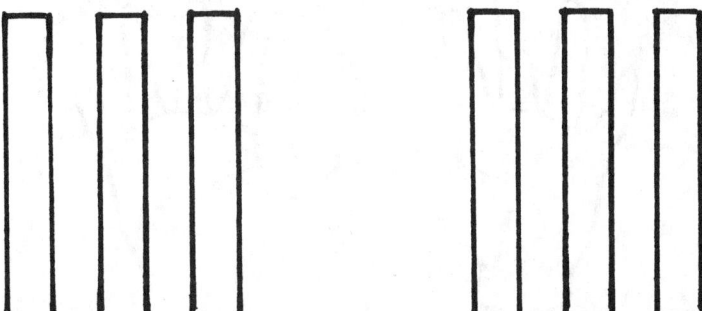

Three plus three is six;
Learn to add with counting sticks.

3

Doubles

Little Book (cont.)

4 + 4 = 8

Four plus four is eight;
I think you're doing great.

4

5 + 5 = 10

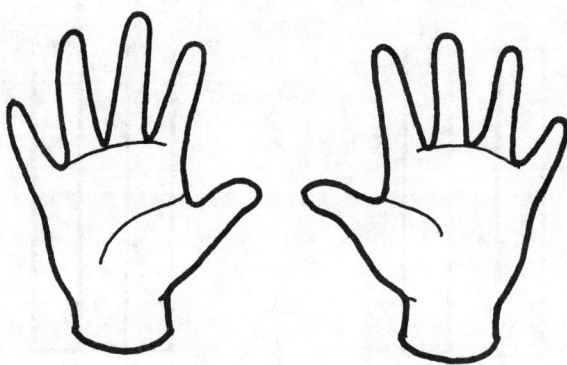

Five plus five is ten;
Let's go back and start again.

5

Doubles

Little Book (cont.)

$$1 + 1 = 2$$
$$2 + 2 = 4$$
$$3 + 3 = 6$$
$$4 + 4 = 8$$
$$5 + 5 = 10$$

Show what you have learned.

Doubles

Patterns

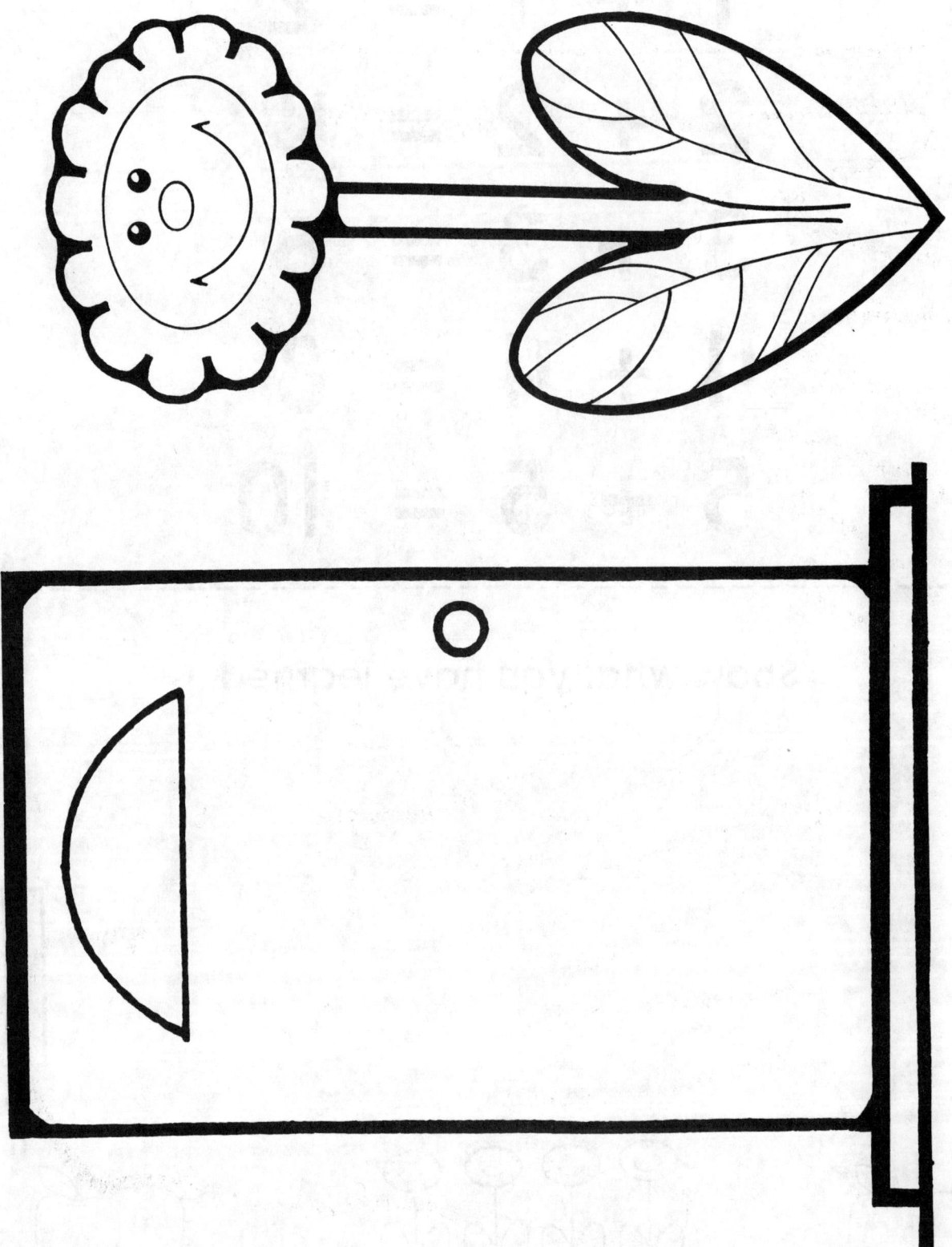

Doubles

Patterns *(cont.)*

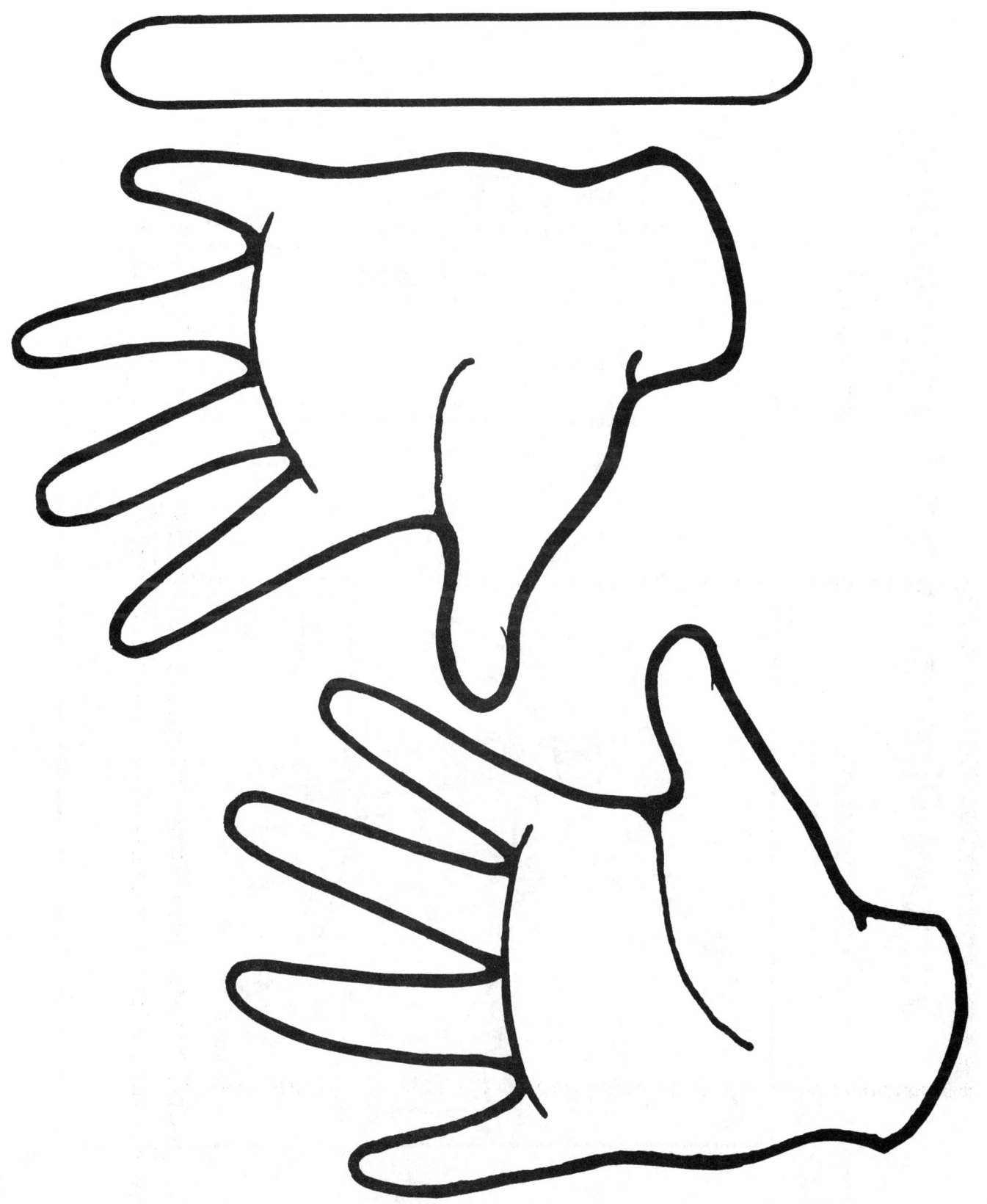

Doubles

Name _____

School Playground Background

As your teacher reads you problems, move the items you collected on the nature walk to solve problems.

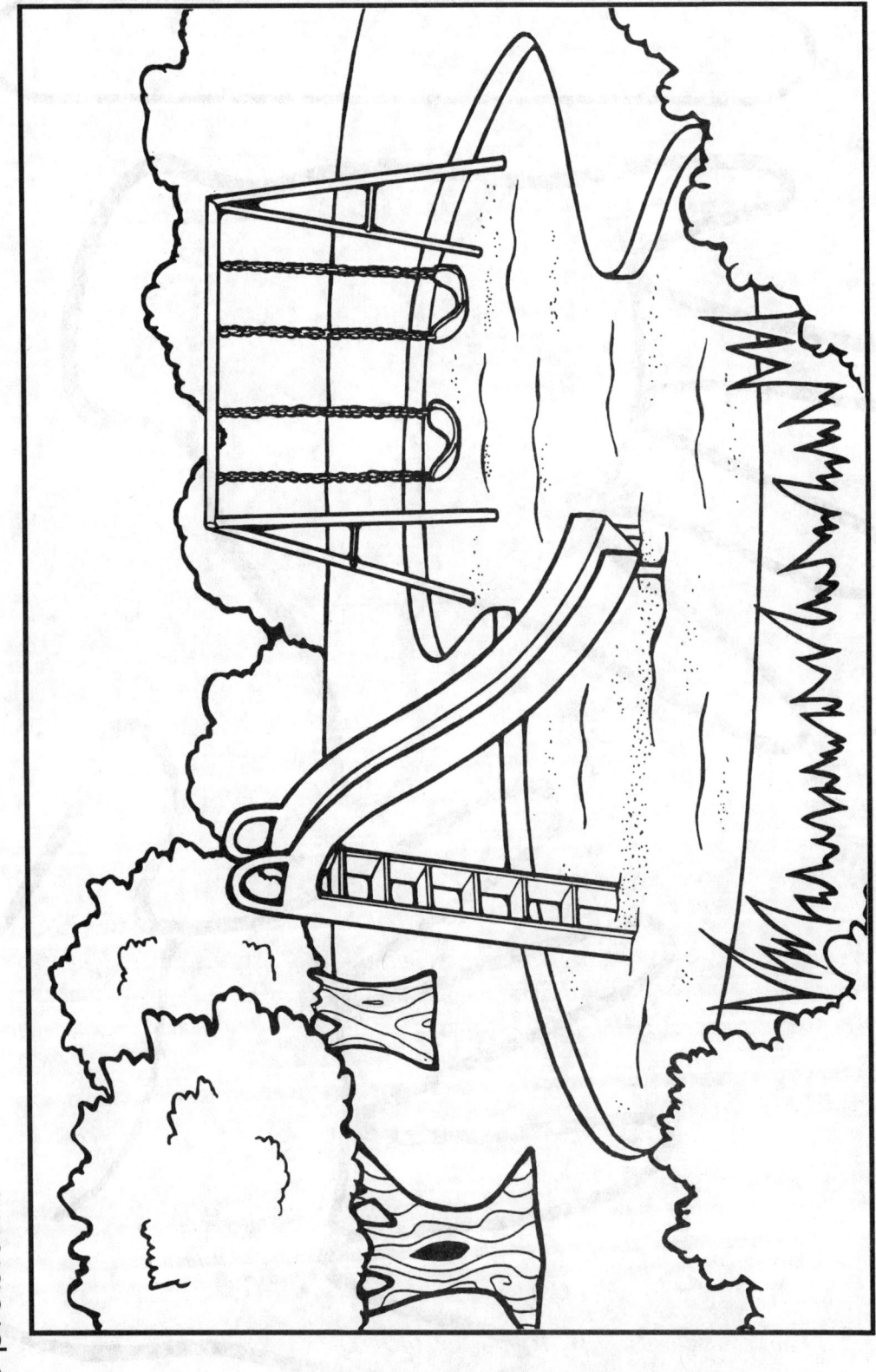

Doubles

A Class Act

A good way to provide repetition without boredom is to have small groups of children act out problems for the class. After each dramatization, the teacher writes the complete problem on the chalkboard. Later, let students attempt to dictate the number sentence to the teacher. Examples:

Have the children act out the problem by motioning with their arms for the other two to come over. One of the students can hold a baseball. This problem will work for other sports as well. Let the children hold a basketball, football, etc.

Two children wanted to play baseball. They decided it would be more fun if they could find two more children. They saw 2 children across the street and called them to come over and play. How many children are playing now?

Use stuffed animals or dolls from the dramatic play center. Cars or zoo animals from the block center can also be used. A third child can play store clerk. Substitute names of children in your class for Susie and Kim.

Susie and Kim went to the toy store. Susie bought 3 toys and Kim bought 3 toys. How many toys did the girls buy?

Use a seasonal theme. In this case spring is used.

Have the children act out growing by being curled up on the floor as a tiny seed. Then sprout by standing; arms uncurl and wave about for leaves. Smile a big smile to blossom. Or students could hold paper flowers. Some can flap arms to be birds or butterflies.

First, 5 daffodils popped out in the spring sunshine. Then 5 tulips burst out. How many flowers grew in the spring?

A silly snake was sliding and slithering along in the spring grass. He was very lonely. Then he met another snake who became his best friend. Now how many snakes are sliding and slithering through the grass? Instruct 2 children to lie on their stomachs and wiggle, while hissing loudly and sticking out their tongues.

In the spring, 3 birds flew in from the south to look for worms. They met 3 birds who were singing about worms. How many birds were there altogether? Have 3 children flap their arms and make pecking motions while the other 3 flap their arms and chirp.

Two worms saw the birds and ran to hide. When they got to the hole, they were surprised by 2 more worms trying to hide. How many worms were in the hole? Have 4 children wiggle across the floor and get behind a desk or bookshelf.

Many butterflies return from Mexico in the spring. There are butterflies everywhere. Amy (or insert a student's name) saw 5 butterflies visiting flowers and then she saw 5 more. How many did she see?

Doubles

Interfacing Addition Cards

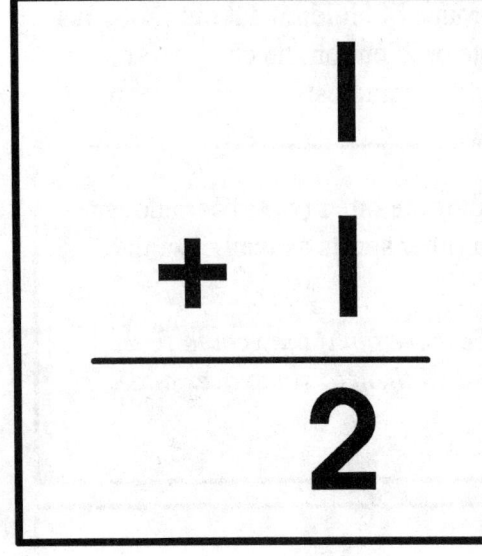

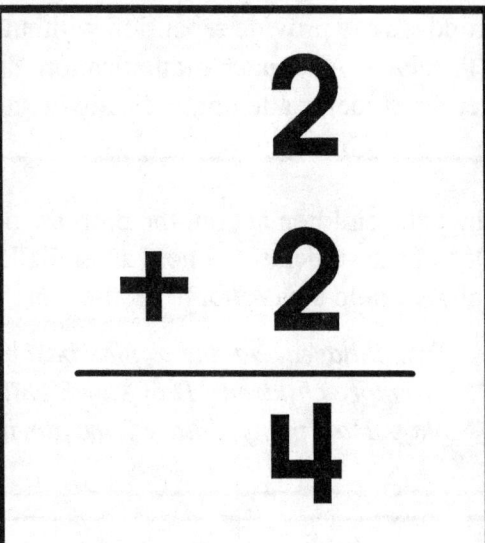

$$\begin{array}{r}3\\+\ 3\\\hline 6\end{array}$$

$$\begin{array}{r}4\\+\ 4\\\hline 8\end{array}$$

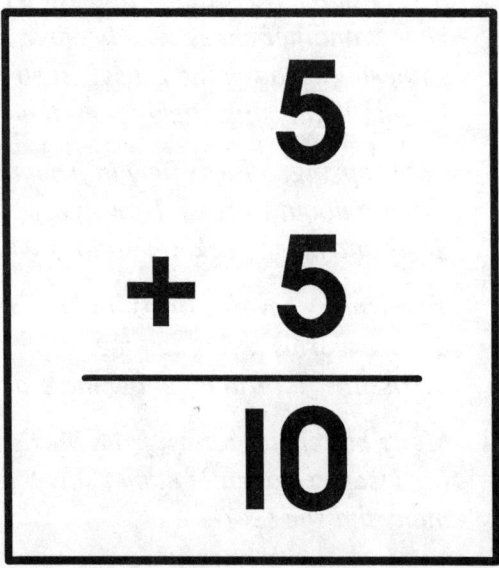

Doubles

Name:_____

Doubles Match

Directions: Cut on dotted lines. Complete the equation by gluing the correct sum next to the addends. (Match the answers to the problems.)

1 + 1 =	2
3 + 3 =	4
5 + 5 =	6
2 + 2 =	8
4 + 4 =	10

©1993 Teacher Created Materials, Inc. #200 Whole Language Units for Math

Adding One

I'm so smart;

I learned a trick,

An easy way

To add things quick.

One plus a number,

Any number plus one,

Is just like counting.

It's easily done.

One plus one is two;

Count on up, is what you do.

Two plus one is three;

It's easy as can be.

Three plus one is four;

Just count on up one more.

Four plus one is five;

I'm the smartest kid alive!

$$1 + 1 = 2$$
$$2 + 1 = 3$$
$$3 + 1 = 4$$
$$4 + 1 = 5$$

by Sandra Merrick

Adding One

Sample Lessons

This unit is a continuation of "Doubles."

Day 1: Introduce the poem using a transparency of page 128. Students ready to read can construct their own Little Books by cutting page 128 into strips and matching text to the equations given at the bottom. This activity should be done in small groups.

Prepare a chart with all the "+1" facts in order or simply write them on the chalkboard. Begin with 1+1=2 through 9+1=10. Help children to notice that the answers sound like counting. Reread this chart after reading the poem each day. After several days, just write the equations on the chalkboard and have students write the answers.

Day 2: Tell flannel board stories. Prepare interfacing addition cards on page 130. Make up stories for the flannel board using patterns from throughout this book. Examples: Johnny took 1 apple to school in his lunch box. His friend gave him 1 more. How many apples does he have now? Eddie ate 3 pieces of cheese. He took another piece of cheese away from a mouse and ate it. How many pieces of cheese did he eat? After each, show the appropriate interfacing card.

Make a number line. Use a long strip of bulletin board paper or craft paper. Students take turns acting out "+1" problems as the teacher writes them on the chalkboard. Have the student read the equation after he/she acts out the problem.

Day 3: Complete worksheets. Use flannel board figures and interfacing numeral cards to demonstrate page 131. Then have the children cut out the numerals and glue them to the correct equation.

The worksheet on page 132 can be demonstrated on the chalkboard. The teacher should complete the first two equations and let students complete the remaining problems. Instruct children to cut out the numerals and glue them in the correct boxes.

At this point, zero as an addend should be introduced. Just have students repeat: *Adding zero to any number does not change it.* Demonstrate with equations and manipulatives.

Use page 133 for evaluation. It serves as a test for both Doubles and Adding One.

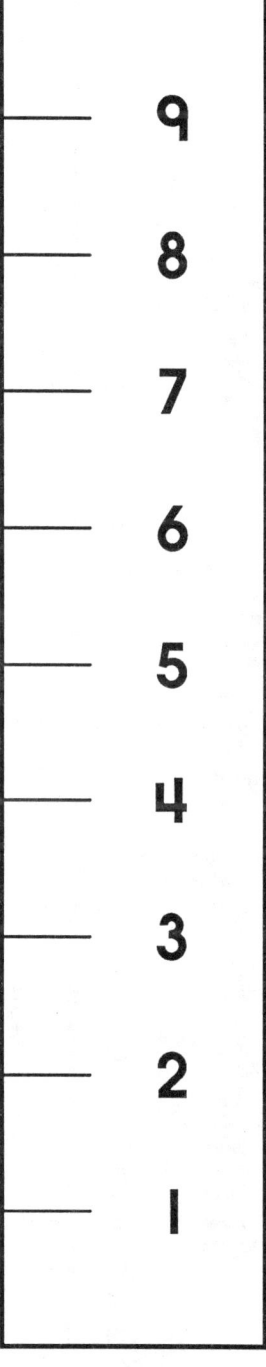

Number Line

Adding One

Interfacing Addition Cards

Make these cards out of interfacing.

$\begin{array}{r}1\\+\ 1\\\hline 2\end{array}$	$\begin{array}{r}2\\+\ 1\\\hline 3\end{array}$
$\begin{array}{r}3\\+\ 1\\\hline 4\end{array}$	$\begin{array}{r}4\\+\ 1\\\hline 5\end{array}$
$\begin{array}{r}1\\+\ 2\\\hline 3\end{array}$	$\begin{array}{r}1\\+\ 3\\\hline 4\end{array}$
$\begin{array}{r}1\\+\ 4\\\hline 5\end{array}$	$\begin{array}{r}1\\+\ 1\\\hline 2\end{array}$

Name _____

Adding One

Adding One

Cut out the numerals and glue them in the boxes where they belong.

5 3 4 2

Adding One

Name _____

Adding One

2 + 1 = ☐

4 + 1 = ☐

1 + 1 = ☐

3 + 1 = ☐

| 2 | 3 | 4 | 5 |

Adding One

Name _____

Evaluation

2 + 1 = ☐   0 + 1 = ☐

1 + 3 = ☐   3 + 2 = ☐

2 + 2 = ☐   0 + 2 = ☐

4 + 1 = ☐   3 + 0 = ☐

1 + 1 = ☐   1 + 2 = ☐

2 + 0 = ☐   4 + 0 = ☐

2 + 3 = ☐   3 + 1 = ☐

5 + 0 = ☐   0 + 3 = ☐

1 + 4 = ☐   0 + 4 = ☐

1 + 0 = ☐   0 + 5 = ☐

More Queen of Hearts
Adapted from Mother Goose by Sandra Merrick

The Queen of Hearts,
She made some tarts,
All on a summer's day;
The Knave of Hearts,
He stole the tarts,
And took them clean away.
The queen asked the knave,
"What did you do?"
The knave answered,
"I'll tell you true.
There were five tarts
By the kitchen door;
The king took one,
And then there were four.
There were four tarts
Cooling under a tree;
The prince took one,
And then there were three.

There were three tarts
Some were red, some were blue;
The princess took one,
And then there were two.
There were two tarts
Brown and toasty done;
The dog took one,
And then there was one.
There was one tart
Sitting in the sun;
I took that one,
And then there were none."
The queen did shout,
"My tarts you took!
You all were naughty,
Now YOU can cook!"

More Queen of Hearts

Sample Lessons

Day 1: Introduce subtraction with a Big Book "The Queen of Hearts." If you do not have enough time, make transparencies of the Little Book pages for the overhead. Explain that a tart is a small pie or cookie with a fruit center.

Play Hide Away with the whole class. Write the equations from "The Queen of Hearts" on the chalkboard. Explain that the minus sign means to take away. The word we use for "take away" is "subtraction." Give each student five interlocking cubes. Begin with all cubes joined together. Have them "break off" any number of cubes that they choose and hide them in their desks. Have the children show the remaining cubes by holding them up.

Call on individual students to tell what they did. Example: "I started with five. I took away two and now I have three left." If students forget to tell what number they started with, remind them that they must tell how many they had when they started. If your students do not have desks, they can place part of the cubes behind their backs.

Day 2: Make subtraction cards from interfacing. Use the problems on page 144. Place on flannel board and read to the class. Use cookie or tart manipulatives to demonstrate each subtraction sentence.

Reread "More Queen of Hearts" each day. Prepare a chart or bulletin board containing the equations illustrated to the lower right:

Read the chart each day also. Point out that the answers are similar to counting backwards.

Model this guessing game for the children. Hold up five cubes linked together. Say: "I am starting with five cubes." Then count the cubes out loud. Put your hands behind your back and put one or more cubes in your other hand. Hold up the remaining cubes. Say: "I started with five cubes, and this is how many cubes I have left. Can anyone tell me how many cubes I took away?" Accept several guesses, then show the missing cubes.

Pass out five interlocking cubes to each child in the class. Instruct one child to hide some of the five cubes, then show remaining cubes. Have students guess how many cubes are hidden. Let the student who gives the correct answer be the next one to hide cubes. Continue until interest wanes.

Subtraction Problems

$5 - 1 = 4$

$4 - 1 = 3$

$3 - 1 = 2$

$2 - 1 = 1$

$1 - 1 = 0$

More Queen of Hearts

Sample Lessons (cont.)

Day 3: Some individuals may be ready to read the Big Book to the class. Provide a pointer for the reader. One child may read the entire book. An alternate method would be to have several children read, with each reading just a few lines.

Prepare and read Little Books. Add several blank pages at the end of the Little Books. Encourage children to write equations for events in the story. Example: Two tarts in the sun, the dog took one. How many were left? Children write 2-1=1. They may also draw math pictures to show what happened in the problem. Draw 2 circles to represent tarts; then put an X on 1 circle. This is an illustration for 2-1=1.

Reproduce enough copies of page 143 so that every student in the class has some cookies or tarts. Trim the page so that some students have five cookies or tarts, some have four cookies or tarts, some have three, and some have two. Each student needs markers to cover the cookies or tarts: plastic disks, plastic cubes, or buttons, etc. Challenge each child to cover part or all of his/her tarts or cookies. Then ask each one to write an equation to show what was done. Have some children move to the front of the room and write their equations on the chalkboard while others write on a paper at their desks.

Day 4: Make interfacing "cookie" cards. Draw two, three, four, or five cookies on each "card." Draw an X on one or more cookies. Use a fine point permanent marker to write matching equations on interfacing rectangles. Demonstrate how to match the cookie cards to the interfacing subtraction cards. Place in the math center.

Let students act out the story using the story patterns on pages 141-142. Either make the patterns into flannel pieces or attach craft sticks to make stick puppets. As you read the poem, let the children move the pieces.

Use a deck of playing cards for equations. Take out all the heart cards and show children how to make problems using them. Leave the cards at the math center so children can make up their own equations.

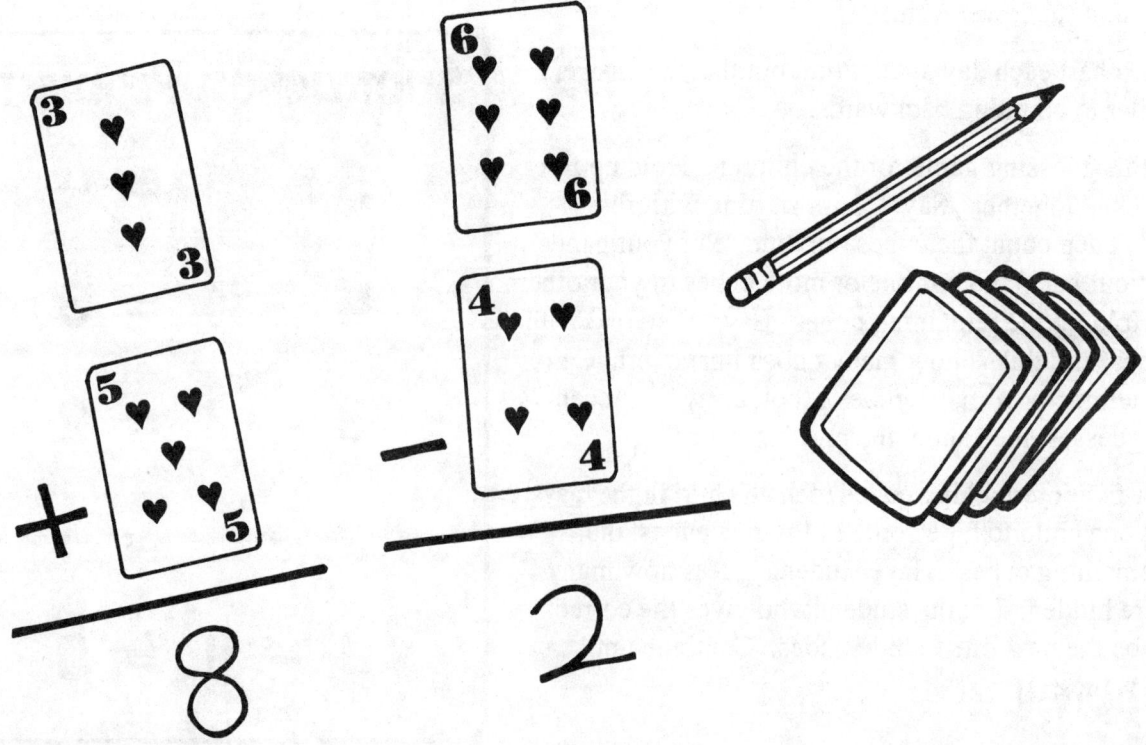

Little Book

My Little Book of
More Queen of Hearts

Name:_____

The Queen of Hearts,
She made some tarts,
All on a summer's day;
The Knave of Hearts,
He stole the tarts,
And took them clean away.

1

The queen asked the knave,
"What did you do?"
The knave answered,
"I'll tell you true.

2

More Queen of Hearts

Little Book (cont.)

There were five tarts
By the kitchen door;
The king took one,
And then there were four.

3

There were four tarts
Cooling under a tree;
The prince took one,
And then there were three.

4

More Queen of Hearts

Little Book (cont.)

There were three tarts
Some were red, some were blue;
The princess took one,
And then there were two.

5

There were two tarts
Brown and toasty done;
The dog took one,
And then there was one.

6

More Queen of Hearts

Little Book (cont.)

There was one tart
Sitting in the sun;
I took that one,
And then there were none."

7

The queen did shout
"My tarts you took!
You all were naughty,
Now YOU can cook!"

8

More Queen of Hearts

Patterns

Use these patterns to act out the "More Queen of Hearts" story, and math games.

©1993 Teacher Created Materials, Inc.

More Queen of Hearts

Patterns *(cont.)*

More Queen of Hearts

Cookie and Tart Patterns

Use for felt cookies and tarts, and/or interfacing strips.

More Queen of Hearts

Name _____

Subtraction Evaluation

3 − 1	4 − 2	2 − 2	5 − 3	3 − 3
5 − 1	3 − 2	4 − 3	5 − 4	2 − 1
4 − 4	5 − 2	1 − 1	5 − 5	4 − 1
2 − 1	1 − 1	3 − 2	5 − 4	4 − 3